T0357203

# THE FISHWIFE COOKBOOK

# THE FISHWIFE COOKBOOK

## DELIGHTFUL TINNED FISH RECIPES FOR EVERY OCCASION

BECCA MILLSTEIN &
VILDA GONZALEZ

PHOTOGRAPHS BY REN FULLER

ILLUSTRATIONS BY DANNY MILLER

HARVEST
An Imprint of WILLIAM MORROW

Thanks to Sara Tane, Jade Qiu, Alex Kelikian, Sam Sujo, and Marie Wright for their recipe contributions in the book.

THE FISHWIFE COOKBOOK. Copyright © 2025 by Rebecca Millstein. All rights reserved. Printed in Malaysia. No part of this book may be used or reproduced in any manner whatsoever without written permission except in the case of brief quotations embodied in critical articles and reviews. For information, address HarperCollins Publishers, 195 Broadway, New York, NY 10007.

HarperCollins books may be purchased for educational, business, or sales promotional use. For information, please email the Special Markets Department at SPsales@harpercollins.com.

FIRST EDITION

Coauthor: Vilda Gonzalez
Designed by Tai Blanche
Photographs by Ren Fuller
Photo assistant: Ty Ferguson
Illustrations by Danny Miller
Food styling by Caroline K. Hwang
Food styling assistant: Jessica Darakjian
Prop styling by Aneta Florczyk
Prop styling assistant: Tom Begandy

Library of Congress Cataloging-in-Publication Data has been applied for.

ISBN 978-0-06-338252-7

25 26 27 28 29 cos 10 9 8 7 6 5 4 3 2 1

We dedicate this book to the folks
who fish, farm, trim, skin, season,
smoke, and hand-pack so that all of us
can enjoy the wonders of tinned fish

# CONTENTS

**Introduction**
ix

**Pantry Essentials**
xiv

**Building Blocks**
1

**Just a Quickie**
13

**A Meal for One**
27

**Summertime**
**59**

**Dinner Is Served**
**95**

**In Front of
the Fireplace**
**121**

**Hosting a
Cocktail Party**
**149**

**Late Night**
**173**

**Sunday Morning**
**189**

**Acknowledgments**
**208**

**Index**
**210**

# INTRODUCTION

The seed that eventually grew into Fishwife was sown when I was twenty-one and spending the weekend in Lisbon, a short plane ride from Granada, where I was living for the fall. My friend and I spent that weekend walking the cobblestone streets, looking up at the tessellated tiles shining on the sides of every building.

We ate mostly in "snack bars," the ubiquitous white-walled, paper-tableclothed restaurants that dot the streets of Lisbon. What the snack bars lacked in décor, they made up for in the quality of their simple dishes. Fresh sea bass with steamed potatoes and broccoli, plastic baskets of warm table bread with soft packets of butter. Large decanters of vinho verde for two euros. A small ceramic dish with a pool of green olive oil in the center, and atop it four silvery boquerones laid out. I dipped a piece of bread into the olive oil, draped the fresh anchovies on top, and took a sip of wine from a small glass. I had never heard of boquerones, but I immediately loved them: bright and vinegary at first, then yielding to a deep savoriness in the second bite.

On the last day of the trip, I was walking by myself through the city and came across some small shops on the waterfront. Through the glass front door of one of them, I saw rows of colored boxes on the shelves, and at first I thought it was a toy shop. When I walked inside, I found that they were not toys at all, but tiny, perfectly narrated tins of fish.

Seven years later, I'm looking out over the production line of a third-generation family-owned anchovy and tuna conserveria in Santoña, Spain, where Fishwife's first anchovy production run is taking place. The whole cannery is filled with a rich, bready scent, earthy and complex like wine. We look out on the cannery's interior from the top of the stairs—me, Fishwife's operations director, and two descendants of the man who built the cannery three generations prior. From up here, you can see the plant in its cavernous entirety, cleaved cleanly into areas dedicated to each step of the production process. Each station is manned by an expert—at one, an older man who triple-cleans the anchovies in hot water; at another, a younger man dries them out by rolling them tight in a cheesecloth. Nearby, there's the long steel table where the anchovies are clipped and cut before being walked over to an even longer table, stretching some one hundred feet down the length of the packing room.

In this room, rows of women—only women are deemed skilled enough to hand-pack the minuscule fillets—perform the final cleaning, then smooth out each individual anchovy, nestling it into its final resting place by hand. Once a tin is filled with eight to ten sparklingly pink anchovies, it's filled to the brim with Spanish extra virgin olive oil and sealed shut. The smell throughout the whole building is warm and almost sweet, nothing like you'd ever imagine an anchovy cannery smelling.

It's not just Spain where women reign supreme in the cannery hall. We travel to the north coast of Scotland to visit the cannery where our mackerel and brisling sardines are packed, and there too the most senior women are revered for their technique. They train the younger staff, who can almost never perfect the steady, patient rhythm of the packing.

On the coast of Washington State in a micro-cannery a tenth the size of the ones in Spain and Scotland, this rule breaks down. A young woman oversees the entirety of production, but it's mostly men—fathers and sons who live in the wooded coastal area—who cut and hand-pack the small fillets of smoked salmon and smoked trout one by one into our tins.

The first cannery I visited after starting Fishwife was on the coast of Oregon, and it had a smokehouse that looked just like you'd imagine it should, with a large, black hand-built kiln the size of a tall man with his arms outstretched. If you opened the smokehouse doors, smoke drifted out, the fire crackled, and you could see alderwood burning beneath the trout and salmon, slowly caramelizing their tender flesh over a period of hours.

Every cannery we partner with has its own distinct character, written in its tastes and smells: its particular machinery, the fish coming in and out the door, and the land and oceans outside. The people move differently. Some are mostly still, moving only their hands and heads as they work, while others rock back and forth on the balls of their feet. Some of the workers began packing fish in their garages as children (it used to be commonplace in the Spanish region of Cantabria to pack anchovies at home); others are new to the job.

But a couple of elements run through all these places. While there are varying degrees of automation—machines that skin coho salmon, ones that chop albacore tuna—the work is hard, shockingly manual, and intricate, and what comes out the other side of the cannery is nothing short of a miracle: a small tin of fish, preserved for years in its most perfect state.

The canneries do the hard work so that when the tinned fish arrive on your plate, you have to do very little. In this book, we've tried to honor each cannery's work and invite the dishes to complement and bring forth the artistry in the tin.

Which brings us to the recipes. In running a tinned-seafood business, I enjoy a front-row seat to all the ways that folks eat tinned fish in their everyday lives. I watch as art imitates life, life imitates art—we write recipes and witness our customers serving them to friends, family, themselves. And we see home cooks create dishes featuring our tins, dishes that never even occurred to us and that we feel compelled to share with our community. This book is a result of that back-and-forth, full of the recipes our community embraced and those that the community brought forward. Vilda Gonzalez, the brilliant cook and writer who has been developing gorgeous Fishwife recipes for years, took on the daunting task of synthesizing all of this dialogue, stirred in with her own rich history with tinned fish (growing up in Sweden eating smoked mackerel on the stoop of the local fish hall; surviving living in New York City as a seventeen-year-old, where the utilitarian, affordable ease of a tin of fish felt like gold; and even navigating health hiccups by leaning on the impressive amount of anti-inflammatory omega-3s in a tin of sardines), into a unified collection of recipes. The chapters are organized by occasion—when I think of some of my favorite tinned fish meals, they're intertwined with place and circumstance. I've enjoyed tinned fish meals in so many places—on my back porch in the summertime, during a road trip up the California coast, and at a full dinner table spilling over with wine, potato chips, and cheese rinds. We imagine the same may be true for you—so, when you're heading to a picnic, a cocktail party, or a brunch, we've made it easy for you to know exactly which chapter to flip to.

That being said, when there's tinned fish involved, you don't have to be headed anywhere to create a sense of occasion. A lunch of sourdough toast, sliced-up peaches or tomatoes, a half-moon of cheese, and a tin of anchovies can transport you—even when enjoyed between Zoom meetings on a Tuesday in February while sitting inside your apartment in Milwaukee.

Tinned fish is magic for a thousand reasons. Because it eliminates the entire process of cooking a fish. Because you can get a shocking 30 grams of protein in a 3.5-ounce tin. Because it can sit in your cupboard for years and still be at its best on its fifth birthday. Because a tremendous amount of love and labor went into the creation of each tin. Because each tin tells an entirely different and unique story of the waters it's from and the cannery in which it was packed.

And last but not least, it's magic because tinned fish makes your life better, easier, more exciting, and more joyful. We created each of these recipes to make this all the more true. Now grab your baguette, butter, Castelvetrano olives, flaky sea salt, and a little glass of chilled wine— it's tinned fish time.

Becca Millstein

# PANTRY ESSENTIALS

Here's our cheat sheet of essentials to keep on hand in your kitchen to ensure a never-ending supply of great tinned fish meals. With these essentials on hand, you'll be able to fix yourself something delicious with little notice. A steaming bowl of white rice with Kewpie mayonnaise and tuna, a piece of buttered toast with anchovies, a simple salad with smoked mackerel and a squeeze of lemon. The best things in life are simple.

## Extra Virgin Olive Oil

High-quality olive oil is the lifeblood of our kitchen. We use it abundantly and often, and you'll find it listed in the vast majority of the recipes in this book. When selecting olive oil, we always make sure it's extra virgin and try to ensure that its harvest date is within a year and a half, at most, at the time of our purchase.

## Fine Sea Salt

All the recipes in this book have been tested and developed using fine sea salt. We find that this type of salt is the most utilitarian, as the fine salt crystals will easily dissolve and incorporate into any recipe—this is especially useful when the recipe doesn't introduce heat. If you prefer using kosher salt, or have a particular brand that you love, please don't feel the need to change your preference for us. The most important thing with

salt is familiarity; different brands of salt have varying levels of salinity, so choose the salt you love and stick with it. Also of important note is that many recipes in this book don't call for a specific amount of salt. Tasting your food as it cooks is a fundamental tenet of ensuring that the final product will be as delicious as possible, so we often encourage you to season, taste, and adjust as you go.

## Flaky Sea Salt

We love to finish dishes with a pinch of flaky sea salt for a pop of crystalline salinity. Our go-to brands are Maldon and Jacobsen Salt Co.

## High-Quality Vinegars

There's a whole world of options when it comes to vinegar, and we certainly encourage you to explore it with curiosity! However, when it comes to what's always in our pantry, we take a no-frills approach: there's white wine vinegar, red wine vinegar, rice wine vinegar, and sherry vinegar. White wine vinegar is great for more delicate applications, like a vinaigrette for tender greens. Red wine vinegar is more assertive, and as such is useful for more assertive applications: Use it to deglaze a pan, to dress heartier greens, or to add a balancing note of brightness to any richer dishes. Rice wine vinegar is a true kitchen workhorse, imparting a clean, neutral acidity whenever used. Sherry vinegar is lovely for imparting a more nuanced, nutty tone to vinaigrettes, marinades, and stews.

## Lemons

We'd be nowhere without the sweet, sunshiny brightness of lemons in our cooking. Our recipes rely heavily on a squeeze of lemon here or there to season, but the true unsung hero is the floral quality of the zest. When shopping for lemons, always opt for organic if you plan on using the zest.

## Pasta

Our pantry is always stocked with a variety of different pasta shapes to help ensure that an impromptu dinner is only a boiling pot of water away. When shopping for pasta, quality is key! We prefer brands whose pastas are made with stone-milled wheat and bronze-die extruders.

## Bread

A good loaf of crusty sourdough will forever have our hearts. We love it with a generous schmear of butter and a tin of fish, but we also rely on it heavily throughout this book for toasts, sandwiches, and a late-night grilled cheese.

## Butter

While olive oil is our go-to cooking oil, we cherish butter for its sweet decadence. We stock our fridge with both salted and unsalted butters. Unsalted is our go-to for cooking; salted is our go-to for slathering on crusty bread. As with all things, quality is key: We recommend sourcing butter that's made from milk from cows raised on pasture.

## Rice

A simple bowl of steamed rice is a tin of fish's best friend. We keep our pantry stocked with long-grain white rice, such as jasmine or basmati, as well as sushi rice.

## Herbs

In our opinion, fresh herbs belong with most meals! We always keep our fridge stocked with a rotating roster of herbs, but parsley, dill, and cilantro are constants. While fresh herbs are our go-to for adding a pop of green, we also love using dried herbs— especially thyme and oregano.

## Eggs

We often turn to eggs to complete our meals, whether it be a jammy egg on a rice bowl, a fried egg adorning anchovy-braised greens, or homemade aioli. We always opt for large pasture-raised eggs, and we try to buy them from our local farmer's market whenever we can.

## Capers

The soft, briny chew of a caper is an invaluable component of any tinned fish lover's pantry. They can quickly uplevel a tinned fish snack plate but also add a savory complexity to pasta sauces, toasts, or salads. The recipes in this book were all developed with non-pareil brined capers. If you're using salt-cured capers, soak them in warm water for at least 10 minutes and rinse well before using.

## Toasted Nuts and Seeds

Toasted nuts and seeds add an inimitable crunch to salads, pastas, soups, you name it! Here at Fishwife, we're big proponents of texture and flavor, so we reach for a toasted nut or seed to add dimension to a dish. We always have almonds, hazelnuts, walnuts, pumpkin seeds, and sesame seeds on hand.

## Chile Flakes

We rely on a few different varieties of chile flakes and powders to add nuance and heat to our dishes. A little pinch of something spicy can help to add depth and dimension to a dish. We keep our pantry stocked with Aleppo pepper (a mild, fruity chile powder that's great for all-purpose use), Urfa chile (a dark, resinous dried chile powder that's great for imparting a fruity, smoky depth), and red pepper flakes to add a straightforward pop of heat to all matter of dishes. We source smoked red pepper flakes from Daphnis and Chloe; simply opening up the jar evokes the feeling of sitting next to a smoky fire.

fresh, traceable spices are Burlap & Barrel, Diaspora Co., and Daphnis and Chloe.

## Kewpie Mayonnaise

While we certainly encourage you to try your hand at making mayonnaise from scratch (we teach you how in this book!), we also fully recognize that there's no replacing the addictively umami-loaded Kewpie mayonnaise, a Japanese brand that uses only egg yolks, unlike American brands, which use the entire egg. There's nothing quite like it. We use it to add a luscious savory quality to rice bowls, hand rolls, and quick toasts.

## Single-Origin Spices

As a company who puts flavor first, we can't overstate our love for a pantry brimming with spices. And as a company whose values are deeply rooted in building meaningful, sustainable relationships with our purveyors, we make it a priority to support other small businesses whose ethos is also deeply committed to integrity within the supply chain. Our favorite places to source flavorful,

## Soy Sauce

A dash of soy sauce can uplevel a bowl of steamed rice and a tin of fish into a craveable meal with ease. It's also an amazing ingredient to have on hand for adding a depth of flavor to pan sauces, stews, or cooked vegetables. When shopping for soy

sauce, we always make sure to stay away from those with unnecessary additives or preservatives.

## Furikake

Furikake is a Japanese seasoning that typically consists of sesame seeds and seaweed. We love to use it to add a pop of texture and flavor to jammy eggs, steamed rice, and hand rolls. We've even been known to generously sprinkle it into a tin of sardines and mackerel and eat it directly from the can.

## Tinned Fish

We'd be remiss if we didn't mention the obvious: A pantry filled with a variety of tinned fish is essential if you're looking to follow the recipes in this book. While we admit to bias for Fishwife tinned fish (and have created most of these recipes with our own tins in mind), there is a glorious world of tinned seafood brands out there for you to discover. We adore Ekone's meaty smoked oysters, Salmon Sisters' rosy wild Alaskan smoked salmon, Patagonia's garlicky lemon herb mussels, Island Creek Oysters' cockles in brine, Güeyu Mar's chargrilled razor clams, Ortiz's buttery ventresca tuna, and Donostia's octopus in olive oil. You'll find recipes that call for tinned fish products that Fishwife doesn't carry—please try out the wares of these purveyors and add them to your rotation.

# BUILDING BLOCKS

Beyond what you can always find stocked in our pantry and fridge, there are certain foundational recipes that we turn to time and time again to either enhance or complete a meal or to jazz up a tin of fish in a moment of need. Many of the recipes in this book rely on these recipes, so we encourage you to take the time to familiarize yourself with them and keep them at the ready to make a delicious meal all the more achievable!

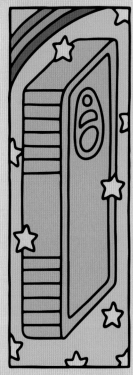

# Building Blocks

Aioli / 3

Olive Oil Fried Bread / 4

Seasoned Labne / 6

Pickled Onion / 7

Steamed Rice / 8

Anchovy Sourdough Breadcrumbs / 9

A Simple Green Salad / 10

Perfectly Jammy Eggs / 11

# AIOLI

Making aioli from scratch shouldn't feel like an intimidating task, as it's a much easier endeavor than you might think. A heavy bowl is the trick, as a flimsy one will spin uncontrollably and make emulsification difficult. We particularly love the spicy, grassy note that olive oil imparts in this aioli, but if you'd prefer a less flavorful version, feel free to opt for a neutral-flavored oil, like grapeseed oil, in its place.

**MAKES 1 SCANT CUP**

1 large garlic clove

3 tablespoons fresh lemon juice

1 large egg yolk

1 teaspoon Dijon mustard

Fine sea salt

¾ cup extra virgin olive oil, or as needed

**RECIPE NOTE:** If you don't have a pantry stocked with mayonnaise and feel inclined to make your own, simply follow this recipe but omit the garlic.

Finely grate the garlic clove into a small bowl. Cover with the lemon juice and set aside to macerate for at least 5 minutes.

Meanwhile, place the egg yolk, mustard, and a generous pinch of salt in your heaviest bowl. Whisk to combine. Now, drop by tiny drop, add your olive oil, whisking constantly with your other hand. As you continue slowly adding the oil, you'll notice that the mixture will become gradually paler and thicker. Once this initial stage of emulsification has been tackled, you can start adding the olive oil in a gentle, steady stream, still whisking all the while! Keep adding oil until your aioli is too thick to continue whisking with ease. You will be impressed by how much oil one single egg yolk can hold. The recipe calls for ¾ cup of olive oil, but you may need to use less or more depending on the size of your egg yolk.

Add the lemon-macerated garlic to this thick emulsion and whisk to combine. Taste and adjust the seasoning with another pinch of salt, if necessary.

Store the aioli in an airtight container in the fridge for up to 2 days.

# OLIVE OIL FRIED BREAD

Good bread is one of life's greatest pleasures, and there are so many ways to enjoy it. Sometimes we enjoy ours torn straight from a warm loaf, adorned with a fat pat of butter and a plump anchovy; other times we enjoy it charred on a grill, and relish the almost burnt edges; sometimes we want what we're serving alongside the bread to take center stage, and in those moments, we rely on the plain simplicity of bread toasted in the toaster. If, however, we had to pick a favorite way to toast and eat our bread, it would be like this: doused in olive oil and fried till golden brown and crunchy on both sides, ready to be adorned by any manner of toppings.

Your favorite sourdough bread, cut into thick slices

A generous glug of olive oil

Heat a skillet over medium-high heat.

Drizzle a thick-cut slice of sourdough in olive oil on both sides, and fry until golden brown on both sides, 2 to 3 minutes per side. Repeat with more slices, as needed.

# SEASONED LABNE

In its simplest form, labne is strained full-fat yogurt that's ubiquitous in many Middle Eastern cuisines. Its texture is akin to cream cheese, which is why it's often referred to as "yogurt cheese." While you can certainly find a tub of labne at a well-stocked grocery store, making your own couldn't be easier. We season ours with a bit of lemon and garlic, but you can always keep yours plain if you want a more versatile result.

**MAKES 1 GENEROUS CUP**

1 quart plain full-fat
  Greek yogurt
2 garlic cloves
Juice of ½ lemon
Fine sea salt

**RECIPE NOTE:** You'll be left with a considerable amount of whey, the tangy liquid that's being strained out of the yogurt. Whey is delicious taken as a probiotic shot, can be used in baking, and is an excellent base for fruity ice pops!

Set a colander over a large bowl. Line the colander with a thick layer of cheesecloth, or use a nut-milk bag or clean tea towel. Pour the yogurt into the cheesecloth and fold the edges of the cheesecloth over the yogurt. Set a plate or any object that could function as a light weight on top of the covered yogurt. Set aside to strain until the texture is akin to cream cheese, 4 to 6 hours depending on the weight of your chosen object. If you're in a rush, you can speed this process along by using more weight to weigh down the straining yogurt.

When the strained yogurt has reached the desired consistency, use a Microplane to grate the garlic into a small bowl and cover with the lemon juice. Set this aside to macerate for 5 minutes. Remove the strained yogurt from the cheesecloth and add to the bowl of macerated garlic. Season with a generous pinch of salt and stir well to combine. Taste for seasoning. Store the labne in an airtight container in the fridge for up to 1 week.

# PICKLED ONION

Having a jar of pickled onion on hand can quickly help to elevate a tin of fish into a balanced meal. A bowl of steamed rice and a tin of mackerel? Add a small pile of pickled onion to add brightness and crunch. Bringing a baguette, labne, and a tin of salmon with you to a picnic? Adorn each bite with a bit of pickled onion for a balancing pop of acid. Needless to say, there are so many potential bites awaiting in your future that could benefit from the small amount of effort that stocking your fridge with pickled onion requires.

**MAKES 1 CUP**

1 red onion, thinly sliced

¾ cup red wine vinegar

¼ cup filtered water

1 bay leaf

1 teaspoon sugar

1 teaspoon sea salt

¼ teaspoon freshly ground black pepper

3 juniper berries (optional)

Place the sliced red onion in a mason jar or other heat-proof container with a tight-fitting lid.

In a medium pot, bring the vinegar, water, bay leaf, sugar, salt, pepper, and juniper berries to a gentle boil over medium-low heat, then remove from the heat and pour over the onion slices. Cover with a lid and set aside to pickle at room temperature for 2 hours.

Transfer to the fridge to pickle for at least another 4 hours before using. These can be stored for upward of a month in the airtight container in the fridge, so long as the pickled onion remains submerged in the brine.

# STEAMED RICE

A simple bowl of steamed rice is a match made in heaven for tinned fish, especially for fattier species like our smoked mackerel or salmon. While we certainly believe in the merits of a rice cooker (and absolutely encourage you to use yours!), a perfect pot of steaming rice can be easily achieved on the stovetop.

**MAKES 3 CUPS**

1 cup white rice
1½ cups filtered water

Place the rice in a colander and rinse with cold water until the water begins to run clear. This step helps remove excess starch from the rice and prevents it from clumping together.

If you have a rice cooker, add the rice and filtered water to it and press that magical button. If you don't have a rice cooker, add the rice and filtered water to a small pot and bring to a boil over high heat. Once boiling, reduce the heat to the lowest simmer and cover the pot with a lid. Cook for 18 minutes, and don't lift that lid!

Take the pot off of the heat. Quickly remove the lid and place a clean tea towel over the pot, then cover again with the lid. Set the pot aside to rest like this for 5 minutes more. The resting time and tea towel help the rice absorb any remaining steam in the pot, which helps prevent the rice from getting gummy. Remove the lid and gently fluff the rice with a fork.

# ANCHOVY SOURDOUGH BREADCRUMBS

A well-stocked pantry is not complete without breadcrumbs. While we certainly condone the use of good old-fashioned panko, we also strongly believe that homemade breadcrumbs are superior when it comes to achieving the best flavor, especially when made with a delicious loaf of sourdough bread. Instead of seasoning our breadcrumbs with salt, we lean on the briny punch of our oil-packed Cantabrian anchovies to deliver an addictive hit of umami. These breadcrumbs are great for adding a pop of texture to salads, roasted vegetables, gratins, pastas—you name it!

**MAKES 1 GENEROUS CUP OF BREADCRUMBS**

¼ cup extra virgin olive oil

4 oil-packed Fishwife Cantabrian Anchovies, finely chopped

3 cups diced sourdough bread

Preheat the oven to 325°F. Line a baking sheet with parchment paper.

In a small skillet, heat the olive oil and anchovies over medium-low heat. Use a wooden spoon to stir the anchovies and evenly distribute them. They will melt into the olive oil as it warms up. Once the anchovies have fully broken down, transfer the anchovy-infused oil to a large bowl. Add the bread pieces and toss in the warm oil until they are thoroughly coated in fat.

Transfer the bread to the baking sheet, and evenly spread out the pieces. Bake for 20 to 25 minutes, until the bread is golden brown and fully dried out.

Transfer the toasted bread to a food processor and blitz until the breadcrumbs resemble pebbly sand. Store in an airtight container in the pantry for up to 1 month.

# A SIMPLE GREEN SALAD

In our dictionary, a simple green salad is a heaping pile of the most delicious tender lettuces you can get your hands on, dressed judiciously in an effortless garlicky vinaigrette. This type of salad holds the power of turning most any dish into a complete meal. In a pinch, dinner can be a simple green salad adorned with your favorite tin of fish. We urge you to shop for your salad greens from a local farmer, as they often grow a much more diverse array of varieties than your standard grocery store might carry. For the sake of ease and fewer dirty dishes, we encourage you to make the vinaigrette in a bowl that's large enough to hold all the greens that you'll be dressing.

**SERVES 2 TO 4**

1 garlic clove

1 tablespoon red or white wine vinegar, plus more to taste

Fine sea salt and freshly ground black pepper

¼ cup extra virgin olive oil

5 ounces tender salad greens

Soft herbs of your choosing, such as dill, parsley, or tarragon (optional)

Use a Microplane to finely grate the garlic into a large bowl. Cover the garlic in the vinegar and set aside to macerate for at least 5 minutes. This process helps to take the raw edge off the garlic. Season this mixture with a pinch each of salt and pepper. Add the olive oil and whisk until the vinaigrette thickens noticeably.

Add the salad greens and herbs, if using, to the bowl, and gently toss the greens in the vinaigrette. Taste a leaf—it should be flavorful with a mild garlicky kick and a pleasant brightness from the vinegar. Adjust the seasoning with an additional pinch of salt or splash of vinegar, if needed.

# PERFECTLY JAMMY EGGS

There are a couple of important things worth noting when it comes to preparing a perfectly jammy egg. First of all, there will be a notable difference in cook time if you are using eggs straight from the fridge versus eggs at room temperature. This timing is for room-temperature eggs, which is what we suggest you use unless you want to risk your cold egg exploding on contact with the hot water. If you're in a rush, you can quickly bring cold eggs to room temperature by placing them in a bowl of warm water for 5 minutes. Next, no two eggs are exactly the same! Use your best judgment regarding the size of the eggs you're using— if they're larger than average, cook for an extra 30 seconds; if they're smaller than average, cook for 30 seconds less. Finally, if you're boiling more than the suggested number of eggs at one time, it's important to factor in that the larger quantity of eggs will cause a bigger drop in the temperature of your boiling water. When boiling large batches of eggs, place a lid on the pot after dropping in the eggs to help expedite the amount of time it takes for the water to return to a boil, and add another 30 seconds to the total cook time.

**MAKES 4 TO 6 EGGS**

4 to 6 large eggs, preferably pasture-raised, at room temperature

Flaky sea salt

Bring a medium pot of water to a boil, then lower the heat ever so slightly before gently dropping your eggs into the water. Cook for 6½ minutes. While the eggs are cooking, prepare an ice bath by filling a large bowl with ice and cold water. When your timer goes off, immediately use a slotted spoon to transfer the eggs into the ice bath; this step helps to halt the cooking process and makes the eggs easier to peel.

When ready to serve, take the eggs out of the ice bath, peel, and slice in half. Season with a pinch of flaky sea salt.

**RECIPE NOTE:** For a perfectly hard-boiled egg, cook for 9 minutes total.

# JUST A QUICKIE

This is our most utilitarian chapter, so get ready to get down to brass tacks. While we love a luxurious evening spent with a few freshly popped tins of fish and ice-cold glasses of vermouth, sometimes we need to sling a satiating meal down our gullets as quickly as humanly possible. And that's what this chapter is for—the grab-n-goes, the five-minute lunches, the survival snacks.

Thankfully, these quick snacks are also some of the best tinned fish has to offer. We can't wait for you to whip them up in record time.

# Just a Quickie

Avocado and Sardine Toast / 15

Radish, Butter, and Anchovy Toast / 16

Tuna and Preserved Artichoke Snack Plate / 19

Sardines with Honey Mustard and Crackers / 20

Deep Dive: The Five-Minute Snack Plate / 21

Seaweed Snacks with Chili Crisp Salmon, Mayo, Scallions, and Sesame Seeds / 22

Smoked Salmon Dip with Crackers / 24

# AVOCADO AND SARDINE TOAST

Here we are, gracing you with another opportunity to eat avocado on toast. We have one big suggestion for upleveling the classic: Gently mash a tin of sardines on a deeply golden piece of bread before you layer on your sliced and seasoned avocado. You'll be left with a heartier, more meal-worthy version.

**SERVES 1**

1 avocado

Juice of ½ lime

Flaky sea salt

Smoked red pepper flakes

1 slice Olive Oil Fried Bread (page 4)

1 tin Fishwife Sardines

Cut the avocado in half and remove the pit. Scoop the flesh out of its peel and lay it flat side down on your cutting board. Thinly slice the avocado and then fan it out by gently pressing down on the slices with the palm of your hand. Season with the lime juice, a generous pinch of flaky sea salt, and smoked red pepper flakes to taste.

When your bread is cool enough to handle, smoosh the sardines onto the toast with the back of a fork. Top the sardines with the sliced and seasoned avocado, and relish in the joys of a simple and speedy meal!

# RADISH, BUTTER, AND ANCHOVY TOAST

There's little more satisfying than the textural balance of a piece of toast, a thick layer of butter, the crunch of a radish, and the meatiness of a plump anchovy. This is less a recipe and more an invitation to indulge in a simple pleasure. Do make sure to let the fried bread sufficiently cool before slathering it in butter, or the butter will immediately melt and you'll miss the softness of its texture.

**SERVES 1**

Salted butter, at room temperature

1 slice Olive Oil Fried Bread (page 4)

5 or 6 English breakfast radishes, thinly sliced

Flaky sea salt

2 or 3 oil-packed Fishwife Cantabrian Anchovies

Chives, thinly sliced

Generously butter the bread, then layer on the radishes until you can't see the surface of the toast. Season with a small pinch of flaky sea salt, drape with the anchovies, and shower it in chives.

# TUNA AND PRESERVED ARTICHOKE SNACK PLATE

This is the dish to call upon when your friends decide to show up for an impromptu dinner, or when you've forgotten to make yourself lunch, or if you have a late reservation and want a pre-dinner snack. Leaning on a well-stocked pantry, all you really need is a tin of tuna, a jar of artichokes, and some Calabrian chile paste. Combine it all on a plate, add some herbs and lemon zest for extra credit, and, in five minutes, you've got a bite that is much greater than the sum of its parts.

**SERVES 4**

Pinky-size dab
  of Calabrian chile paste

1 teaspoon lemon juice,
  plus the zest of ½ lemon

1 tablespoon extra virgin
  olive oil

4 or 5 best-quality
  preserved artichoke
  hearts, quartered

1 tin Fishwife
  Albacore Tuna

Torn fresh basil leaves

Flaky sea salt and freshly
  ground black pepper

To make the dressing, combine the Calabrian chile paste, lemon juice, and olive oil in a small bowl and whisk to emulsify.

Assemble the quartered preserved artichoke hearts on a plate and nestle bite-size pieces of tuna on them.

Drizzle the dressing over the top. Garnish with the basil, lemon zest, a pinch of flaky sea salt, and black pepper to taste.

# SARDINES WITH HONEY MUSTARD AND CRACKERS

One of the great joys of being a tinned fish fanatic is bonding with other fanatics about their favorite ways to cook with a tin of fish. As our whole world revolves around tinned fish and recipes featuring it, it's always a very welcome treat to be met with the excitement of somebody else's recipe. Friends of ours mentioned the quick bite that's on constant rotation in their home: a tin of sardines and homemade honey mustard on a Wasa cracker. Wasa crackers are a Swedish-style crispbread that can be found in most large grocery stores. If you can't get your hands on them, feel free to sub in your favorite crackers. We recommend seeded or rye-based crackers.

This dish is a perfect balance of meaty, spicy, crunchy, and sweet—a combination worthy of being anyone's go-to. If you fall in love with the flavor of this simple homemade honey mustard, we recommend making a big batch to keep on hand for any emergency snacking needs. Keep the ratio of the recipe the same, and scale up to your heart's content.

**SERVES 1**

2 tablespoons whole-grain mustard

2 teaspoons honey

2 Wasa crackers

1 tin Fishwife Sardines, drained

In a small bowl, mix the whole-grain mustard and honey until combined, then smear it generously on the Wasa crackers. Top with the sardines.

**RECIPE NOTE:** If making a larger quantity of honey mustard, keep any leftovers in an airtight container in the fridge for up to 2 weeks.

# DEEP DIVE
## THE FIVE-MINUTE SNACK PLATE

THE SNACK PLATE HAS MANY NAMES — IT'S BEEN CALLED GIRL DINNER, SNACK BOARD, GRAZING BOARD — BUT IT'S UNMISTAKABLE IN ITS SIMPLICITY & ITS DELICIOUSNESS. TO PUT TOGETHER THE PLATONIC IDEAL OF A SNACK PLATE, SIMPLY FOLLOW THE INSTRUCTIONS BELOW.

## STEP 1

PICK 1 OF EACH:
- TINNED FISH
- FRUIT
- VEGETABLE
- BREAD OR CRACKER
- DIP OR SPREAD (BUTTER & OLIVE OIL COUNT)
- CHEESE

## STEP 2

ASSEMBLE ON A PLATE, CUTTING BOARD, OR IN A SHALLOW BOWL

## STEP 3

POUR YOURSELF A COOL GLASS OF SPARKLING WATER OR WINE & ENJOY!

# SEAWEED SNACKS WITH CHILI CRISP SALMON, MAYO, SCALLIONS, AND SESAME SEEDS

This quick and satisfying bite was born from a desire to transform the classic prepackaged seaweed snack into a more sustaining but equally convenient one. If you have a pantry stocked with all the listed ingredients, the only active prep required is to slice enough scallions to adorn each bite with a pop of green. Easy!

**SERVES 1 TO 2**

5 or 6 sheets seaweed snacks

2 tablespoons Kewpie mayonnaise

1 tin Fishwife Smoked Salmon with Sichuan Chili Crisp

1 tablespoon toasted sesame seeds

2 to 3 tablespoons thinly sliced scallions

Spread out the seaweed snacks on a plate. Layer bite-size amounts of mayonnaise, salmon, sesame seeds, and scallions onto each piece of seaweed. Fold it up like a taco and devour.

# SMOKED SALMON DIP WITH CRACKERS

This salmon dip comes together in a jiffy with the help of a trusty food processor. Simply add in the ingredients and whizz them up until the texture becomes creamy and lush. Enjoy as a quick snack on the go or as a light, simple lunch. This dip pairs well with crackers but is also delicious with a plate of fresh-cut vegetables.

**SERVES 1 AS A MEAL, OR 4 AS A LIGHT SNACK**

⅓ cup cream cheese

¼ cup mayonnaise

¼ cup sour cream

1 tin Fishwife Smoked Atlantic Salmon

2 tablespoons capers, coarsely chopped

1 tablespoon chopped fresh chives

Zest of 1 lemon

Fine sea salt and freshly ground black pepper

A few fresh dill sprigs, for garnish

Crackers or fresh-cut vegetables, for serving

In a food processor, blend the cream cheese, mayonnaise, and sour cream until combined. Add the smoked salmon, capers, chives, lemon zest, and a small pinch each of salt and pepper. Pulse a couple times, until combined. You're not going for the texture of a puree, so be careful not to overmix. The ideal texture should be thick and spoonable with small bite-size pieces of salmon evenly distributed throughout. Transfer to a small bowl and garnish with a few sprigs of dill. Serve with crackers or vegetables.

# A MEAL FOR ONE

Here, we imagine you on a Friday afternoon with some spare time to play with and a well-stocked fridge and cupboard. You're looking to stir up a meal that'll feed your soul. You're going to light a candle on your kitchen table, crack open a book, and treat yourself kindly. These are elegant, nutritious, and simple meals that will leave you feeling deeply satiated. These recipes can *also* be easily multiplied to serve a friend, a partner, or some kiddos.

# A Meal for One

Avocado, Sardine, and Urfa-Spiced Pepita Salad / 30

Cherry Tomato Tartine with Aioli and Smoked Salmon / 32

Matcha Ochazuke with Smoked Salmon / 34

Deep Dive: The Weeknight Tinned Fish Bowl / 36

Spanish Tortilla with Smoked Salmon, Crème Fraîche, and Hot Sauce / 39

Caesar Wedge Salad with Anchovy Breadcrumbs / 41

Trout Salad Sandwich / 43

Radicchio Salad with Fennel, Toasted Walnuts, and Rainbow Trout / 44

Asparagus Rice Bowl with Salmon, Toasted Almonds, and Herbs / 47

Sardine and Marinated Zucchini Sandwich / 50

Tonnato with Charred Broccoli, Pickled Onion, and Anchovy Breadcrumbs / 53

Hand Roll with Smoked Salmon, Avocado, and Cucumber / 55

# AVOCADO, SARDINE, AND URFA-SPICED PEPITA SALAD

This salad is simple enough to whip together when you're up against the clock and need a nutritious meal, but it's also delicious enough to proudly serve to friends. The key to this recipe is to season all the respective components before tossing everything together in a big salad bowl.

**SERVES 1**

**FOR THE URFA-SPICED PEPITAS**

¼ cup pumpkin seeds

½ teaspoon extra virgin olive oil

¼ teaspoon Urfa chile (or more if you're a sucker for a kick)

Fine sea salt

**FOR THE SALAD**

1 avocado

Juice of 1 lime

Flaky sea salt

3 to 4 ounces tender salad greens

1 tablespoon extra virgin olive oil

1 tin Fishwife Sardines, drained and broken into bite-size pieces

**MAKE THE URFA-SPICED PEPITAS:** Heat a small skillet over medium-low heat. Place the pumpkin seeds in the pan and toast until golden and aromatic, 2 to 3 minutes, tossing the pan occasionally to make sure they don't burn. Add the olive oil, Urfa, and a small pinch of sea salt, toss to coat, then take off the heat. Coarsely chop the mixture and set aside.

**PREPARE THE SALAD:** Cut the avocado into bite-size pieces and season with a squeeze of lime and a pinch of flaky sea salt. Add the salad greens to a large bowl. Season with the juice of 1 lime (sans what you used to season the avocado) and another pinch of flaky sea salt. Toss to properly coat the greens, then drizzle in the olive oil and toss again.

Add the sardines, seasoned avocado, and the ¼ cup Urfa-spiced pepitas.

# CHERRY TOMATO TARTINE WITH AIOLI AND SMOKED SALMON

This is the holy grail of summertime toast. The flavor palette is a riff on the foundational principles of a BLT: the savory smoked salmon, rich aioli, and juicy tomatoes are evocative of the classic. And while there's no lettuce in sight, fresh marjoram provides the necessary hit of green. Enjoy for breakfast, or cut the toast into quarters and serve as a side dish or appetizer at your summer cookout. Note that the aioli requires the most preparation of any component in this recipe, so start by making a batch before embarking on the rest.

**SERVES 1 VERY HUNGRY INDIVIDUAL, OR 2 AS A MODERATE LUNCH**

½ pint cherry tomatoes, halved

Flaky sea salt and freshly ground black pepper

1 teaspoon extra virgin olive oil

Small splash of red wine vinegar

2 slices Olive Oil Fried Bread (page 4)

¼ cup Aioli (page 3)

1 tin Fishwife Smoked Atlantic Salmon

3 to 4 fresh marjoram sprigs (in a pinch, substitute fresh oregano)

In a medium bowl, combine the halved cherry tomatoes with a generous pinch of flaky sea salt, an even more generous grinding of black pepper, the olive oil, and vinegar. Toss to combine, then taste-test a tomato. The objective here is to season the tomatoes in a way that allows them to taste more like themselves, by adding just enough salt, spice, and acid to really make their flavor pop.

To assemble, generously smear the fried bread with a thick layer of aioli. Arrange the macerated tomatoes on top and nestle in a few pieces of smoked salmon. Finish with the fresh marjoram and another grind of black pepper.

# MATCHA OCHAZUKE WITH SMOKED SALMON

## by Jade Qiu

Smoky tinned salmon and earthy matcha make this classic Japanese comfort food a well-balanced treat. Prepare the savory awase dashi ahead of time—or use powdered dashi in a pinch—for a cozy late-night snack or light breakfast that can be stirred up in minutes. Top with roasted sesame seeds and serve with crunchy pickled cucumbers or tangy umeboshi (preserved ume plums) to add a vibrant textural dimension to the dish.

**SERVES 1, WITH PLENTY OF LEFTOVERS**

### FOR THE AWASE DASHI

1 piece dried kombu

1 packed cup dried bonito flakes

### FOR THE MATCHA OCHAZUKE

1 teaspoon matcha powder

2 teaspoons mirin

1½ teaspoons soy sauce

Kosher salt (optional)

1 tin Fishwife Smoked Atlantic Salmon, flaked

1 cup Steamed Rice (page 8)

Roasted sesame seeds, julienned shiso leaves, and shredded nori, for garnish

Japanese pickles (umeboshi, pickled cucumber, pickled daikon), for serving

**MAKE THE AWASE DASHI:** In a small pot, combine the kombu and 4 cups of water and bring to a low simmer over medium-high heat. Remove the kombu before the mixture reaches a full boil. As the pot simmers, add in the bonito flakes, stirring occasionally until the mixture comes to a boil. Cook for 1 to 2 minutes, then take the pot off the heat and let the dashi steep for 10 minutes.

Strain the dashi and discard the solids. Once cooled, any leftover dashi can be stored in an airtight container in the fridge for up to 1 week.

**MAKE THE MATCHA OCHAZUKE:** In a small bowl, whisk the matcha with a generous splash of hot, but not boiling, water (around 175°F) until it is blended and foamy. In a measuring cup, pour in the matcha, warm dashi, mirin, and soy sauce. Stir to combine. Season with salt to taste, if desired.

Divide the smoked salmon evenly on top of 2 bowls of rice, and pour the matcha broth all over. Top with sesame seeds, shiso leaves, nori, and whatever else you prefer. Serve with pickles alongside.

# DEEP DIVE
## THE WEEKNIGHT TINNED FISH BOWL

THE TINNED FISH BOWL HAS SAVED OUR LIVES (AND OUR BELLIES!) ON COUNTLESS BUSY WEEKNIGHTS. THE TINNED FISH BOWL CONSISTS OF A GRAIN BASE, A VEGETABLE, A TINNED FISH OF YOUR CHOICE, AND A SAUCE OR DRESSING TO TIE IT ALL TOGETHER.

## GRAIN
RICE, PASTA, COUSCOUS, WHEAT BERRIES

## TINNED FISH
SARDINES, TROUT, SALMON, TUNA, ANCHOVIES

## VEGGIES
BROCCOLI, SPINACH, AVOCADO, PEPPERS, MUSHROOMS

## SAUCE
CHILI CRISP, TOMATO SAUCE, OLIVE OIL

# SPANISH TORTILLA WITH SMOKED SALMON, CRÈME FRAÎCHE, AND HOT SAUCE

Let us preface this recipe by saying that there are many passionate schools of thought regarding what constitutes the perfect tortilla: a golden exterior or a blond exterior; meltingly soft potatoes or almost al dente potatoes; a runny center or a dense, set center. As with most things, there is no definitive right or wrong—just preference. Try, taste, try, and taste again to figure out what you enjoy most. With that said, this technique results in a small tortilla with golden blisters and a soft, just-set interior. Tinker as you must to find your sweet spot.

**SERVES 1, WITH PLENTY OF LEFTOVERS**

⅔ cup extra virgin olive oil

5 golf-ball-size waxy potatoes (like Yukon Gold), peeled and diced into ½-inch pieces

1 tennis-ball-size yellow onion, diced

1 bay leaf

1½ teaspoons fine sea salt

5 large eggs

Heaping spoonful of crème fraîche, for serving

1 tin Fishwife Smoked Atlantic Salmon, for serving

Green hot sauce, like El Yucateco, for serving

Chopped fresh chives, for garnish (optional)

In an 8-inch nonstick skillet, heat the olive oil over medium heat. Add the potatoes, onion, bay leaf, and 1 teaspoon of the salt. Stir to combine, snugly nestling all the potato pieces under the olive oil. Reduce the heat to medium-low and cook for 10 to 15 minutes, until the potatoes are fork-tender. Do be careful not to let things get too hot; we're not looking to get too much color on the onion or the potatoes.

While the potatoes are cooking, place the eggs and remaining ½ teaspoon salt into a medium bowl and whisk well. Once the potatoes are cooked, take the pan off the heat and use a spider skimmer or slotted spoon to transfer the cooked potatoes to the whisked eggs. Stir to combine. Strain the remaining oil in the skillet into a container and save for later use; this is liquid gold!

RECIPE CONTINUES >

Return the pan to the stove over medium heat. Add 1 tablespoon of the reserved olive oil to the pan. When hot but not smoking, pour in the potato and egg mixture. With a spatula or wooden spoon, stir as though you are scrambling eggs. Continue to tuck the edges in to prevent the eggs from overcooking. When the eggs are just barely set (this should take roughly 3 minutes, but use your judgment), take the pan off the heat and place a large plate facedown over the pan. Grip the pan's handle tightly with one hand and hold the plate tightly over the pan with the other. Flip the tortilla from the pan onto the plate, then slide the now-face-up tortilla back into the pan to cook for another minute or so. Depending on the design of your pan, you might want to use a spatula to even out the top of the tortilla and to tuck in the sides to make a more taut circle. When cooked to your liking, remove from the heat and set aside to cool for at least 10 minutes.

To serve, place a slice of tortilla on a plate, with crème fraîche, tinned salmon, and hot sauce alongside. Garnish with the chives, if using.

Store leftover tortilla in an airtight container in the fridge for up to 4 days. To reheat, preheat the oven to 350°F, place the tortilla in an ovenproof container, and cook until warmed through, about 5 minutes. Leftovers are also delicious eaten at room temperature.

# CAESAR WEDGE SALAD WITH ANCHOVY BREADCRUMBS

**by Marie Wright**

Caesar salad, but make it wedge! This classic Caesar is elevated by the elegant presentation of two cleanly chopped wedges draped in plump anchovies and scattered with toasted panko. The coolness of the chilled romaine combined with the creamy, umami-rich dressing and the crunchy panko makes this a perfectly refreshing side. When you're ready to eat, slice up the romaine heart and anchovies with a knife and fork, and give it a quick toss.

## SERVES 1 AS A MEAL, OR 2 AS A SIDE

- 1 tin Fishwife Cantabrian Anchovies in Extra Virgin Olive Oil
- ¼ cup panko breadcrumbs
- 2 garlic cloves
- 1 large egg yolk
- 2 tablespoons grated Parmesan cheese, plus more if desired
- 3 to 4 tablespoons fresh lemon juice, to taste
- ¼ cup extra virgin olive oil
- Fine sea salt and freshly ground black pepper
- 1 large romaine lettuce heart, chilled

Open the anchovy tin and drain the oil into a small skillet; set the pan over medium heat. When the oil is hot, add the breadcrumbs and toast, stirring constantly, until golden brown, about 3 minutes.

Remove 6 anchovies from the tin and set aside (to top your lettuce wedges). Put the remaining anchovies into a mortar and pestle. Add the garlic cloves and smash together into a paste. (Alternatively, you can do this on a cutting board and then transfer the paste into a small bowl.)

Add the egg yolk, Parmesan, and lemon juice to the mortar or bowl and whisk together until well combined. Stream in the oil while whisking until the dressing is emulsified. Add salt and pepper to taste.

Cut the romaine heart in half lengthwise and arrange on a serving plate. Drizzle the dressing over the cut side of the halves, scatter the breadcrumbs on top, and drape the reserved anchovies over each half. Grate more Parmesan on top, if desired, and finish with more pepper.

# TROUT SALAD SANDWICH

Almost everyone knows and loves a classic tuna salad, but this trout salad is far from traditional; it trades fennel for celery and tangy labne for mayonnaise. What it lacks in familiarity, it makes up for in flavor and nutrient density. We love ours sandwiched between two pieces of whole-grain bread, but feel free to scale up the recipe and serve it as a dip with crunchy vegetables.

**SERVES 1**

1 small shallot, minced

½ medium fennel bulb, thinly sliced

Zest of 1 lemon, plus 2 tablespoons fresh lemon juice

Fine sea salt and freshly ground black pepper

1 tin Fishwife Smoked Rainbow Trout

⅓ cup labne

1 tablespoon extra virgin olive oil

2 tablespoons finely chopped fresh parsley

2 tablespoons finely chopped fresh dill

Aleppo pepper

2 slices whole-grain sandwich bread

2 or 3 lettuce leaves

In a medium bowl, combine the shallot, fennel, lemon zest, lemon juice, a small pinch of salt, and a grind of black pepper. Set aside to macerate for 10 minutes. Flake in the trout, then add the labne, olive oil, parsley, dill, a small pinch of Aleppo pepper, and another pinch of salt. Mix to combine and taste for seasoning.

Toast your bread in a toaster till golden and crunchy on the outside but still giving and soft on the inside. Load one slice of bread with the trout salad and top the other with the lettuce leaves. Close the sandwich, then cut in half.

# RADICCHIO SALAD WITH FENNEL, TOASTED WALNUTS, AND RAINBOW TROUT

Tinned fish and radicchio are a match made in salad heaven. This salad is crunchy, fresh, and loaded with enough healthy fat and protein to make it a sufficient lunch for one. The key to countering the bitterness of radicchio is to dress it generously in a vinaigrette that balances the chicory's assertive flavors with a touch of sweetness—here, we lean on shallot and honey to do the trick.

**SERVES 1 AS A GENEROUS MEAL, OR 2 AS A SIDE**

1 small shallot, finely minced

1 tablespoon white wine vinegar

Fine sea salt

3 tablespoons extra virgin olive oil

1 teaspoon honey

½ teaspoon Aleppo pepper or other mild fruity ground chile

Freshly ground black pepper

1 small head of radicchio, cored, leaves torn into bite-size pieces

1 small fennel bulb, thinly sliced

⅓ cup toasted walnuts, coarsely chopped

1 tin Fishwife Smoked Rainbow Trout

In a large bowl, combine the shallot, vinegar, and a small pinch of salt and set aside to macerate for 5 minutes. Add the olive oil, honey, Aleppo pepper, and a grind of black pepper. Whisk to emulsify.

Swirl the bowl to coat the internal surface area with the vinaigrette. Add the radicchio and fennel and toss well until every leaf looks glossy. This way of dressing

**RECIPE CONTINUES >**

a salad, essentially dressing the bowl instead of the greens, helps to evenly coat your greens without weighing them down.

Add the walnuts and rainbow trout and delicately toss once more before serving.

# ASPARAGUS RICE BOWL WITH SALMON, TOASTED ALMONDS, AND HERBS

Consider this herb-and-vegetable-loaded rice bowl a celebration of spring's most tender asparagus. This dish comes together quickly, especially if you have leftover steamed rice on hand, and is great enjoyed as a packed lunch on the go. If you're using in-season asparagus, you won't need to cook it for more than a minute or two, as just-harvested asparagus is incredibly tender and sweet. You can find imported or greenhouse-grown asparagus year-round at your grocery store, but note that the stalks will likely be thicker and tougher than its seasonal counterpart. If this is what you're working with, cook the asparagus for a few more minutes than this recipe suggests.

**SERVES 1**

2 tablespoons extra virgin olive oil, plus more for serving

1 small bunch of asparagus, cut into 1-inch pieces, tough ends discarded

Fine sea salt

2 garlic cloves, minced

1 cup Steamed Rice (page 8)

1 tin Fishwife Smoked Atlantic Salmon, flaked into bite-size pieces

¼ cup toasted almonds, chopped

⅓ cup chopped fresh parsley

⅓ cup chopped fresh dill

2 tablespoons capers, coarsely chopped

Zest and juice of 1 lemon

1 teaspoon Urfa chile

Heat a large skillet over medium-high heat. When the pan is hot but not smoking, add the olive oil, asparagus, and a pinch of salt. Cook undisturbed for 1 to 2 minutes, until the asparagus is just al dente,

RECIPE CONTINUES >

then lower the heat a smidge and add the minced garlic to the pan. Cook for another minute, or until the garlic is aromatic. Transfer the cooked asparagus to a large bowl.

Add the rice, salmon, almonds, parsley, dill, capers, lemon zest, lemon juice, Urfa chile, a generous glug of olive oil, and a big pinch of salt to the bowl. Mix well to evenly incorporate all the ingredients. Taste for seasoning and adjust if needed.

# SARDINE AND MARINATED ZUCCHINI SANDWICH

When summer rolls around, zucchini shows up with vigor. If you've ever grown the vegetable yourself, you surely understand this sentiment: What at first feels like a proper welcoming committee for the season's change eventually feels like a relentless glut to handle. This sandwich is the perfect antidote to any zucchini-induced fatigue you might be experiencing. Shaving the vegetable thinly allows it to stay crisp and refreshing, and the long ribbons are a thirsty sponge for the assertive flavors of garlic and za'atar in the marinade. When tucked in between thick-cut pieces of sourdough alongside a tin of sardines and whipped feta, it makes for an exceptionally delicious summer sandwich—and manages to make zucchini feel brand-new.

**SERVES 1**

½ large zucchini, thinly shaved with a vegetable peeler

Fine sea salt

3 tablespoons extra virgin olive oil

1 tablespoon fresh lemon juice

2 garlic cloves, grated

1 teaspoon za'atar

Freshly ground black pepper

½ cup feta cheese, crumbled

2 tablespoons plain full-fat Greek yogurt

2 thick slices of a sourdough country loaf (a sesame seed loaf is especially delicious)

1 tin Fishwife Sardines, drained

1 small handful of fresh parsley leaves

1 generous handful of pea shoots or another hearty microgreen

In a medium bowl, season the zucchini ribbons with a generous pinch of salt—massage it in well, and set the zucchini aside for at least 15 minutes. Salting the

RECIPE CONTINUES >

zucchini helps to draw out moisture, which leaves you with a crisper zucchini that will take better to the marinade.

In a small bowl, combine the olive oil, lemon juice, garlic, za'atar, and a small pinch each of salt and pepper. Whisk to emulsify.

After 15 minutes, the zucchini should be sitting in a puddle of liquid. Pour this off, gently rinse the zucchini of excess salt, and dry any residual moisture off the ribbons with a paper towel. Return the zucchini to the bowl, pour the dressing over it, and place in the fridge to chill and marinate for at least 30 minutes.

Combine the feta and yogurt in a high-powered blender or food processor and whip until smooth and fully combined.

Slather each slice of bread with the whipped feta. Layer one side with the marinated zucchini and the other with sardines. Add the parsley and pea shoots, then close the sandwich like a heavy book. Slice in half to serve.

# TONNATO WITH CHARRED BROCCOLI, PICKLED ONION, AND ANCHOVY BREADCRUMBS

Tonnato is a silky sauce made with a combination of canned tuna, anchovies, and mayonnaise. It's most commonly known to be served alongside cold slices of veal in the classic Italian dish vitello tonnato, but we've fallen for its savory charm as a simple way to spruce up roasted vegetables. Here, we use it to adorn a head of charred broccoli, and lean on fridge and pantry staples like Pickled Onion (page 7) and Anchovy Sourdough Breadcrumbs (page 9) to maximize flavor and texture with minimal effort. This recipe for tonnato makes more than you'll eat in one sitting, so consider it your meal prep! You can slather the addictive sauce on a sandwich, enjoy it as a dip with fresh vegetables for a quick snack, or use it to add a boost of flavor to a grain bowl.

**SERVES 1, WITH PLENTY OF LEFTOVERS**

2 tins Fishwife Albacore Tuna

4 oil-packed Fishwife Cantabrian Anchovies

¾ cup Aioli (page 3), or store-bought mayonnaise in a pinch

1 tablespoon capers

1 tablespoon fresh lemon juice

2 teaspoons Dijon mustard

½ teaspoon freshly ground black pepper

Fine sea salt

1 large broccoli head, cut into bite-size florets

3 tablespoons extra virgin olive oil

¼ cup toasted pumpkin seeds

¼ cup Pickled Onion (page 7)

2 tablespoons Anchovy Sourdough Breadcrumbs (page 9)

**RECIPE NOTE:** The tonnato can be stored in an airtight container in the fridge for up to 3 days.

RECIPE CONTINUES >

Place a baking sheet in the oven. Preheat the oven to 425°F.

Combine the tuna, anchovies, aioli, capers, lemon juice, mustard, and pepper in a food processor. Blend until well combined. Taste for seasoning; as multiple ingredients in this recipe are already inherently salty, you may find that you don't need to add any additional salt. However, if you feel like the sauce's flavor isn't quite popping, add a small pinch of salt to season.

In a large bowl, toss the broccoli in 2 tablespoons of the olive oil and a generous pinch of salt. Remove the baking sheet from the oven and evenly distribute the broccoli on it. Roast the broccoli for about 15 minutes, until the florets are al dente and charred around the edges.

Return the broccoli to the bowl and add the toasted pumpkin seeds, pickled onion, and remaining 1 tablespoon of olive oil. Toss to combine.

Assemble the dish by adding a large puddle of the tonnato to a serving plate, layer on the dressed broccoli, then sprinkle everything with the anchovy breadcrumbs.

# HAND ROLL WITH SMOKED SALMON, AVOCADO, AND CUCUMBER

A hand roll (read: toasted seaweed filled with sushi rice and any manner of savory fillings, rolled into a cone shape that fits perfectly in the palm of your hand) is an approachable method for making sushi at home. The most demanding component of this recipe is cooking the sushi rice; aside from that, you're simply chopping and seasoning vegetables before assembling, rolling, and devouring.

This recipe yields more sushi rice than you'll need for one serving of hand rolls. Use leftovers for a rice bowl or invite over a couple of friends for a roll-your-own-hand-roll lunch.

**SERVES 1 OR 2**

1 cup sushi rice

1½ cups filtered water

3 tablespoons rice wine vinegar

2 tablespoons sugar

½ teaspoon fine sea salt

1 sheet nori, cut in half widthwise

2 teaspoons Kewpie mayonnaise

1 tin Fishwife Smoked Atlantic Salmon

½ avocado, sliced

¼ large cucumber, cut into matchsticks

1 teaspoon furikake

Soy sauce, for serving (optional)

Place the rice in a sieve and rinse with tap water until the water runs clear.

In a small saucepan, add the rice and the filtered water and set aside to soak for 30 minutes. This step will allow the rice to cook more evenly. Once the rice has soaked, bring the contents of the pot to a boil

**RECIPE CONTINUES >**

over high heat. As soon as the water begins to boil, lower the heat to maintain a gentle simmer. Place a tight-fitting lid on the pot and cook for 15 minutes. Quickly peek in the pot to confirm that all the water has been absorbed; if it hasn't, cook for 2 minutes more or until all the water has been absorbed.

Remove the pot from the heat and set aside to rest for 10 minutes. Do not remove the lid or disturb the rice during this resting time.

In a small bowl, combine the rice wine vinegar, sugar, and salt. Once the rice has rested, remove the lid and pour the vinegar mixture over the rice. Use a wooden spoon or paddle to gently and evenly incorporate the seasoned vinegar into the rice.

To assemble the hand roll, lay a half sheet of nori on a clean work surface. Gently spread ¼ cup of the cooked and seasoned sushi rice onto half of the sheet. Layer on 1 teaspoon of the mayonnaise, half of the tin of smoked salmon, half of the avocado slices, half of the cut cucumber, and ½ teaspoon of the furikake. Gently lay the loaded sheet of nori in the palm of one hand. Use your thumb to fold the loaded corner onto itself, then use your other hand to wrap the remaining part of the sheet over the loaded half, creating a cone shape. Gently wet your finger with a few drops of water and run it alongside the seam of nori to help seal it.

Repeat with the other half sheet of nori and the remaining ingredients. Enjoy the hand rolls dipped in soy sauce, if desired.

Summertime—with its glistening produce, chirping crickets, and late sunsets—is one of the loveliest seasons to eat tinned fish, and we look forward to it every year. After all, there is no happier plate than one filled with juicy sardines and a slice of sourdough bread dripping with EVOO-drenched heirloom tomatoes and peaches. Can we get an amen?!

# Summertime

Baguette with Labne, Pickled Onion, and Smoked Salmon / 63

Potato Salad with Green Beans, Goat Cheese, and Smoked Salmon / 64

Pan Bagnat: Niçoise Salad Sandwich / 67

Juicy Summer Tomatoes with Sardines and Caper Aioli / 71

Deep Dive: A Lovely Picnic in the Park / 72

Pasta Salad with Tuna, Roasted Red Peppers, Feta, Red Onion, and Kalamata Olives / 73

Heirloom Tomato, Nectarine, Whipped Ricotta, Anchovy, and Basil Salad / 76

Smoked Mackerel with Smashed Cucumbers and Dill / 77

Chili Crisp Salmon Lettuce Wraps with Pickled Onion and Cucumber / 79

Crispy Potatoes with Herbed Yogurt, Pickled Onion, and Tinned Trout / 80

Heirloom Tomatoes with Garlic Toast and Anchovies / 83

Tuna with White Bean Salad, Fennel, and Preserved Lemon Vinaigrette / 84

Chili Crisp Salmon Burger with Lettuce, Tomato, and Mayo / 87

Rainbow Trout Tacos with Peach and Sungold Tomato Salsa / 90

Chili Crisp Salmon Panzanella / 92

# BAGUETTE WITH LABNE, PICKLED ONION, AND SMOKED SALMON

Imagine this as a deconstructed and (arguably) more elegant rendition of a sour cream and onion dip. This is one of our favorite dishes to bring along for a picnic, as all that's required is slinging all the listed ingredients into your favorite picnic basket (perhaps alongside a bottle of something bubbly?) before heading out for a sunny day in the park.

**SERVES 4**

1 French baguette

⅔ cup Seasoned Labne (page 6)

2 tins Fishwife Smoked Atlantic Salmon

Pickled Onion (page 7)

1 small bunch of dill

To serve, tear off a piece of baguette, generously slather it with labne, then layer on the salmon, pickled onion, and some sprigs of dill.

If serving this dish in a more formal setting, serve the smoked salmon on a platter with slices of baguette, a ramekin of labne, and little piles of pickled onion and dill.

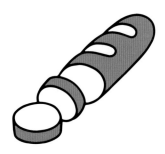

# POTATO SALAD WITH GREEN BEANS, GOAT CHEESE, AND SMOKED SALMON

This salad is a picnic's best friend; it gets better the longer it sits and can be made ahead hours before it's time to meet your friends at the park, so long as you don't devour it before you arrive. Make the vinaigrette in a bowl that's large enough to hold all the salad ingredients for ease of cleanup; that way you can first whisk up the vinaigrette and then build (and even transport) the salad with only one bowl dirtied.

**SERVES 4**

20 small new potatoes, cut in half

8 garlic cloves, coarsely chopped

2 tablespoons extra virgin olive oil

2 teaspoons fine sea salt

1 large bunch of green beans, ends trimmed and cut into 2-inch pieces

¼ cup thinly sliced fresh basil

1 tin Fishwife Smoked Atlantic Salmon

2 ounces soft goat cheese

**FOR THE BALSAMIC AND MUSTARD VINAIGRETTE**

2 tablespoons balsamic vinegar

1 tablespoon whole-grain mustard

2 teaspoons Dijon mustard

1 small pinch of fine sea salt

¼ teaspoon freshly ground black pepper

3 tablespoons extra virgin olive oil

Preheat the oven to 350°F.

In a large roasting pan, combine the potatoes, chopped garlic, olive oil, and 1 teaspoon of the salt. Toss to coat. Roast for 25 to 30 minutes, until the

RECIPE CONTINUES >

potatoes are golden and tender when pierced with the tip of a knife.

Meanwhile, bring a large pot of water to a boil over high heat. Once boiling, season with the remaining 1 teaspoon of salt. Add the green beans and cook for 2 minutes, then take off the heat and strain.

**MAKE THE BALSAMIC AND MUSTARD VINAIGRETTE:** In a large bowl, combine the balsamic vinegar, both mustards, the salt, and pepper. Slowly pour in the olive oil and whisk to emulsify.

Add the roasted potatoes (make sure you add all the roasted garlic from the pan too!), blanched green beans, and basil to the bowl and give it a good mix. Crumble in the tinned salmon and goat cheese, and give it all one more gentle toss.

# PAN BAGNAT: NIÇOISE SALAD SANDWICH

Pan bagnat is everything you love about a classic niçoise salad, only sandwiched in between two pieces of crusty bread. This iconic summer sandwich features both anchovies and tuna, making it a next-level lunch to share with your tinned-fish-loving friends. The key to a proper pan bagnat, beyond the quality of the niçoise salad itself, is the right bread: The proper ratio of crust to crumb is essential, so reach for a crusty baguette or a small ciabatta if you can. This sandwich gets better and better the longer it sits, as all the juices from the filling seep into the sturdy bread, making it the perfect candidate for packing along for a summer road trip or a picnic in the park.

**SERVES 2 FOR A SATIATING LUNCH, BUT CAN BE DEVOURED BY 1 IF YOU'RE ESPECIALLY HUNGRY**

1 large heirloom tomato, sliced

Fine sea salt and freshly ground black pepper

2 oil-packed Fishwife Calabrian Anchovies, minced

2 garlic cloves, minced

2 tablespoons finely chopped kalamata olives

2 teaspoons extra virgin olive oil

1 teaspoon Dijon mustard

1 teaspoon red wine vinegar

A small ciabatta or French baguette, halved

1 tin Fishwife Albacore Tuna, flaked into bite-size pieces

2 large hard-boiled eggs (see Note, page 11), sliced

1 small handful of fresh basil leaves

Season the heirloom tomato slices with salt and pepper. Set aside.

In a small bowl, combine the anchovies, garlic, kalamata olives, olive oil, Dijon mustard, and vinegar. Smear the dressing on both sides of the bread.

**RECIPE CONTINUES >**

On one side of the sandwich, layer on the tuna, seasoned tomato slices, hard-boiled eggs, and basil. Season with a generous grind of pepper, then top with the other slice of bread.

Firmly press down on the sandwich to compact the ingredients and secure all the goodness inside. Slice in half to serve.

# JUICY SUMMER TOMATOES WITH SARDINES AND CAPER AIOLI

You might have noticed by now that we have a thing for the marriage of tomatoes and aioli. We are firm believers that the combination of the two just never gets old, hence . . . another recipe featuring both! Why not?! Here, we add capers to our classic aioli to welcome a briny pop of texture and turn it into a satiating dish with the addition of a tin of sardines. This dish is great eaten with some Olive Oil Fried Bread (page 4) to sop the juices off the plate, but is equally satisfying eaten on its own—so long as you lick your plate clean.

**SERVES 2**

1 small shallot, minced

2 teaspoons sherry vinegar

Fine sea salt

2 large ripe tomatoes, cut into bite-size pieces

2 teaspoons extra virgin olive oil

Flaky sea salt and freshly ground black pepper

2 tablespoons capers, coarsely chopped

1 tablespoon finely chopped fresh parsley

1 scant cup Aioli (page 3)

1 tin Fishwife Sardines

In a medium bowl, combine the minced shallot, sherry vinegar, and a pinch of fine sea salt and set aside to macerate for 5 minutes. This process essentially mimics a quick pickle, softening the shallot's sharp bite while adding a welcome pop of brightness to the dish. Add the tomatoes, olive oil, a generous pinch of flaky sea salt, and a small pinch of black pepper. Toss gently to coat.

In a small bowl, fold the chopped capers and parsley into the aioli, then smear it on the bottom of a serving platter. Using a slotted spoon, plate the marinated tomatoes on top of the aioli. If you don't have a slotted spoon, do your best to leave any extraneous juices that the tomatoes released in the bowl; otherwise you will end up with a puddle on the plate.

Break the sardines into bite-size pieces and nestle them into the tomatoes.

# DEEP DIVE
## A LOVELY PICNIC IN THE PARK

THERE ARE FEW BETTER WAYS TO SPEND A SUMMER AFTERNOON THAN LOUNGING IN A SUNNY PARK ATOP A PICNIC BLANKET, GRAZING ON YOUR FAVORITE SNACKS WITH A DEAR FRIEND OR TWO. HERE'S HOW WE PACK FOR A DELIGHTFUL SUNSHINY PICNIC.

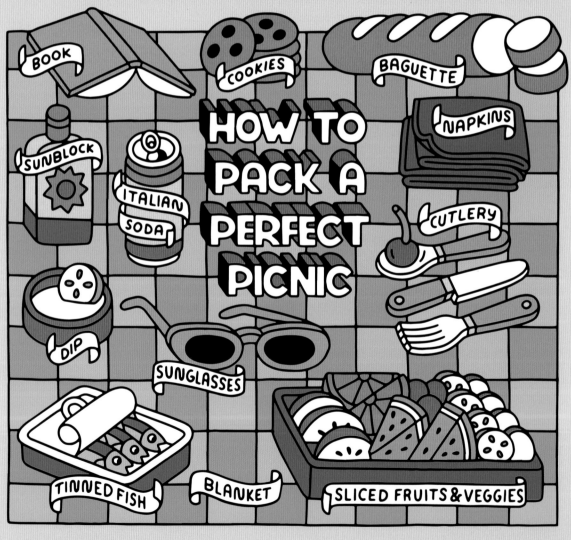

HOW TO PACK A PERFECT PICNIC

BOOK

COOKIES

BAGUETTE

NAPKINS

SUNBLOCK

ITALIAN SODA

CUTLERY

DIP

SUNGLASSES

TINNED FISH

BLANKET

SLICED FRUITS & VEGGIES

# PASTA SALAD WITH TUNA, ROASTED RED PEPPERS, FETA, RED ONION, AND KALAMATA OLIVES

This is the holy grail of pasta salads. Imagine the flavor profile of a Greek salad but with pasta standing in for the tomatoes and cucumbers. Make sure that your pasta is no more cooked than a toothsome al dente, as the pasta will continue to soften as it soaks up all the juices in the pasta salad.

**SERVES 2 OR 3**

Fine sea salt

3 cups dried penne rigate

2 large red bell peppers

½ red onion, thinly sliced

2 garlic cloves, grated

1 tablespoon red wine vinegar, plus more to taste

Freshly ground black pepper

¼ cup extra virgin olive oil

¼ cup pitted kalamata olives

1 tin Fishwife Albacore Tuna, flaked into bite-size pieces

½ cup crumbled feta cheese

½ cup chopped fresh parsley

Bring a large pot of water to a boil. Season generously with salt—you want the water a smidge less salty than the sea. Cook the pasta according to the package instructions, making sure to err on the side of al dente. Strain and rinse with cold water to stop the cooking process, then set aside while you prepare the other components.

Set the oven to broil. Line a baking sheet with aluminum foil. Place the red bell peppers on top, and broil for about 5 minutes per side, until the skin is blistered and black on all sides. Remove from the oven and place the peppers in a container with a lid (or simply a bowl with a plate stacked on top) to continue steaming them. Let them sit for 10 to 15 minutes.

While the peppers are steaming, make the vinaigrette. In a small bowl, combine the red onion, garlic, vinegar, and a generous pinch each of salt and black pepper. Slowly pour in the olive oil and whisk to emulsify.

**RECIPE CONTINUES >**

Once the peppers have properly steamed, their skin should slip right off. Peel both peppers and remove the core and seeds. Cut the roasted peppers into bite-size strips.

Combine the cooked pasta, roasted peppers, olives, tuna, feta, and parsley in a large bowl. Toss to evenly distribute the ingredients, then douse in the vinaigrette. Toss a few more times to make sure every morsel is equitably dressed in the vinaigrette. Take a bite, making sure you have a little bit of everything on your fork, and taste for seasoning. Does it need any more salt? Black pepper? Vinegar? Adjust the seasoning if needed.

# HEIRLOOM TOMATO, NECTARINE, WHIPPED RICOTTA, ANCHOVY, AND BASIL SALAD

## by Alex Kelikian

This dish invites you to showcase the best of summertime produce, replete with fresh nectarine, heirloom tomato, and basil. The salad can be thrown together quickly and served as a simple lunch with crusty bread or as a gasp-inspiring appetizer at a late-summer backyard dinner. This twist on a caprese—adding in the sweetness of the nectarine, the richness of the ricotta, and the brine of the anchovies—is an unadulterated midsummer delight. To guarantee yourself or your guests a succession of perfect bites, we encourage you to make sure there's an equal ratio of tomato to nectarine to basil.

### SERVES 2 TO 4

1 cup ricotta cheese

1 heirloom tomato, sliced

1 nectarine, sliced

1 tin Fishwife Cantabrian Anchovies in Extra Virgin Olive Oil

1 handful of fresh basil leaves

Good-quality extra virgin olive oil

Flaky sea salt

In a food processor or blender, process the ricotta for 30 seconds, or until light and fluffy.

Arrange the tomato and nectarine slices on a large plate. Drape with enough anchovies to provide a savory pop for each bite. Garnish with a generous handful of basil.

If you want to get fancy, pipe your ricotta into squiggles from a pastry bag or a zip-top bag snipped at an angle to add an extra touch to this bright plate. Otherwise, spoon dollops all across the plate, drizzle with olive oil, and finish with a couple pinches of flaky sea salt.

# SMOKED MACKEREL WITH SMASHED CUCUMBERS AND DILL

This is the perfect meal for the hottest days of summer; the smashed and marinated cucumbers are crunchy, refreshing, and flavor-packed, and the meaty smoked mackerel provides sustenance without weighing you down.

**SERVES 4**

2 large cucumbers

1 teaspoon fine sea salt, plus a pinch

⅓ cup extra virgin olive oil

4 large garlic cloves, minced

2 teaspoons red pepper flakes

2 tablespoons rice wine vinegar

⅓ cup chopped fresh dill

⅓ cup chopped scallions

2 tins Fishwife Slow Smoked Mackerel, flaked

Flaky sea salt, to finish (optional)

Cut the cucumbers into bite-size pieces, then gently smash them with the flat end of a knife. This process helps to expose more surface area for flavor to cling to and is also a more interesting shape to eat. Place the cucumbers in a large bowl and toss with the 1 teaspoon fine sea salt. Set aside to allow the salt to draw out the excess moisture in the cucumbers.

Heat the olive oil in a small saucepan over medium heat. Add the minced garlic and cook, stirring occasionally, until the garlic is just starting to turn golden, about 2 minutes. As soon as the garlic has taken on color, take it off the heat immediately, as it will continue to cook and can quickly burn. Stir in the red pepper flakes and a small pinch of fine sea salt.

Drain the excess water from the cucumbers. Add the rice wine vinegar and half of the dill and scallions to the bowl with the cucumbers. Toss well to combine, then add the toasted garlic oil and flaked mackerel and gently toss again to ensure that every nook and cranny gets coated in the flavorful oil. Scatter the remaining herbs over the top and finish with a pinch of flaky sea salt if desired.

# CHILI CRISP SALMON LETTUCE WRAPS WITH PICKLED ONION AND CUCUMBER

These lettuce wraps are an effortlessly impressive summertime snack. If you have a batch of pickled onion at the ready in your fridge, then the assembly of this refreshing and savory bite shouldn't take more than five minutes.

**SERVES 2**

1 tin Fishwife Smoked Salmon with Sichuan Chili Crisp, oil reserved

7 or 8 crisp cup-shaped lettuce leaves, such as romaine or Bibb

21 to 24 cucumber slices, lightly seasoned with flaky sea salt

¼ cup Pickled Onion (page 7)

Lime wedges, for serving

On a large platter, arrange the salmon, lettuce leaves, cucumber slices, a neat pile of pickled onion, and a few lime wedges.

Build the lettuce wraps by nestling a piece of salmon, 3 cucumber slices, and a couple pickled onion slices in a leaf of lettuce. Finish with a squeeze of lime and a drizzle of the oil from the salmon tin.

# CRISPY POTATOES WITH HERBED YOGURT, PICKLED ONION, AND TINNED TROUT

The crisp, crackly edges of a properly roasted potato are one of life's greatest edible pleasures. We could eat a baking sheet's worth like we would a bag of potato chips. If, however, we find the restraint to turn them into a finished dish, this recipe is always the formula we're reaching for. The pickles bring a pleasing pop of acid; the yogurt sauce is cooling, creamy, and herbaceous; and the protein and savoriness from the tinned fish round it out into a proper meal. Feel free to experiment with any tender herbs of your choice for seasoning the yogurt; this recipe suggests a combination of equal parts parsley, dill, and tarragon but would be equally delicious with cilantro and scallions, mint and chives, or a bounty of basil.

**SERVES 4**

8 golf-ball-size Yukon Gold potatoes

1 tablespoon fine sea salt, plus more to season

1 bay leaf

¼ cup extra virgin olive oil

2 garlic cloves

1 tablespoon fresh lemon juice

½ cup plain full-fat Greek yogurt

¼ cup chopped tender herbs (equal parts fresh parsley, dill, and tarragon), plus 1 small handful of whole leaves, for garnish

¼ cup Pickled Onion (page 7)

1 tin Fishwife Smoked Rainbow Trout

Flaky sea salt, to finish

In a medium saucepan, place the potatoes, fine sea salt, and bay leaf. Add enough water to cover the potatoes by a generous inch. Bring to a boil over high heat and cook until the potatoes are easily pierced

**RECIPE CONTINUES >**

by the tip of a sharp knife. Depending on the size and freshness of your potatoes, this can take anywhere from 15 to 35 minutes; a golf-ball-size potato should take about 20 minutes to cook through. Once the potatoes are tender, drain and set aside to cool.

Preheat the oven to 450°F. Line a baking sheet with parchment paper.

When the potatoes have cooled enough for you to handle with ease, gently smash them on a cutting board with a flat surface that's large enough to cover the surface area of the potato—the bottom of a mason jar works great for the job. Arrange the smashed potatoes on the parchment-lined baking sheet. Douse the potatoes in the olive oil, making sure they're evenly coated. Season with a generous pinch of fine sea salt.

Bake for 10 to 20 minutes, then flip the potatoes and cook for 10 to 20 minutes more, until they are deeply golden and crispy around the edges.

While the potatoes are roasting, prepare the yogurt. Use a Microplane to grate the garlic into a medium bowl. Cover the garlic with the lemon juice and set it aside to macerate for 5 minutes. Add the yogurt, herbs, and a generous pinch of fine sea salt to the bowl. Mix to combine and taste for seasoning.

Generously cover the bottom of a serving plate with the herbed yogurt. Layer on the potatoes and top with the pickled onion slices and trout, and garnish with the whole herb leaves. Finish with a pinch of flaky sea salt. As you're plating, make sure there is an appropriate ratio of goodness for every bite.

# HEIRLOOM TOMATOES WITH GARLIC TOAST AND ANCHOVIES

It doesn't get much simpler (or more delicious) than this. Simply rub garlic on some delicious olive oil fried bread, slice a couple ripe tomatoes, present all the components on a beautiful plate, and let your guests do the rest. A fan favorite forever.

**SERVES 2 TO 4**

2 large heirloom tomatoes, cut into thick slices

Flaky sea salt and freshly ground black pepper

2 to 4 slices Olive Oil Fried Bread (page 4)

2 or 3 garlic cloves

1 tin Fishwife Cantabrian Anchovies in Extra Virgin Olive Oil

Season the sliced tomatoes with a pinch of flaky sea salt and black pepper. Do keep in mind that you'll be eating these tomatoes draped in briny anchovies, so use a lighter hand seasoning than you normally might.

Rub each side of the fried bread with the garlic cloves.

Present the seasoned sliced tomatoes on a big platter with the stacked garlic toast and the tin of anchovies. To serve, drape 1 or more seasoned tomato slices on a piece of toast and top with a couple of plump anchovies.

# TUNA WITH WHITE BEAN SALAD, FENNEL, AND PRESERVED LEMON VINAIGRETTE

While we absolutely love cooking beans from scratch, there is a particular satisfaction and sense of ease provided by popping open a good ol' reliable can of beans. In this case, we marry canned white beans with tender albacore tuna, marinated fennel, lots of herbs, and a bright preserved lemon vinaigrette. The flavors improve as the salad rests, making it the perfect dish to pack along for an early-summer picnic or to bring to a potluck.

**SERVES 4**

1 large shallot, thinly sliced

1 fennel bulb, thinly sliced (see Note, page 86)

Zest and juice from 2 lemons, plus more juice to taste

1 teaspoon fine sea salt, plus more to taste

½ teaspoon freshly ground black pepper

1 tablespoon finely chopped preserved lemon peel, or 1 tablespoon preserved lemon paste

2 teaspoons whole-grain mustard

1 teaspoon honey

1 teaspoon red pepper flakes

⅓ cup extra virgin olive oil, plus more to taste

2 tins Fishwife Albacore Tuna

1 (15.5-ounce) can white beans, rinsed and drained

⅓ cup fresh basil, finely chopped

⅓ cup fresh parsley, finely chopped

⅓ cup fresh dill, finely chopped

In a large bowl, combine the shallot, fennel, lemon zest, lemon juice, salt, and pepper. Set aside for at least 10 minutes to give the shallot and fennel enough time to soak up the acid from the lemon juice.

RECIPE CONTINUES >

Add the preserved lemon peel, mustard, honey, and red pepper flakes to the bowl. Slowly add the olive oil in a thin stream and whisk to incorporate. The large pieces of fennel and shallot can be an obstacle for proper emulsification, so don't fret if your vinaigrette doesn't fully come together—so long as the flavors in the vinaigrette are balanced, everything will come together deliciously in the end.

Flake the tuna into bite-size pieces, then add them to the mix, along with the beans and chopped herbs. Gently mix to combine and taste for seasoning. Adjust if necessary with another pinch of salt, squeeze of lemon, or splash of olive oil.

RECIPE NOTE: If you buy a bulb of fennel with a lush head of hair (aka the fragrant fronds that are all too often discarded), please feel free to substitute ⅓ cup of fennel fronds for any of the listed herbs.

# CHILI CRISP SALMON BURGER WITH LETTUCE, TOMATO, AND MAYO

The fattiness of our tinned salmon is a great match for a faux burger, giving the patty that tender, savory quality you crave, while the chili crisp adds an unexpected pop of complexity and spice. Turn to this recipe when you're grilling for friends (pescatarians and meat-eaters alike), or make a smaller batch for yourself when you have an insatiable hankering for a good burger.

**SERVES 4**

2 tins Fishwife Smoked Salmon with Sichuan Chili Crisp

½ large yellow onion, finely chopped

1 small carrot, grated

½ cup panko breadcrumbs

2 garlic cloves, minced

1 tablespoon Dijon mustard

1 tablespoon finely chopped scallions

1 tablespoon finely chopped fresh cilantro (optional)

1 large egg

Grapeseed oil or another neutral oil, for frying

4 slices Swiss or American cheese

Kewpie mayonnaise

4 hamburger buns, buttered and toasted

Sliced tomato, lettuce leaves, and thinly sliced red onion, for serving

In a large bowl, combine the salmon with the chopped yellow onion, carrot, panko, garlic, mustard, scallions, cilantro (if using), and egg. Mix well to combine. Set aside for 10 minutes to allow the panko to hydrate. To test the mixture for the right texture, grab a small

RECIPE CONTINUES >

amount and gently squeeze it in your palm; it should hold together without effort. Shape into 4 burger patties.

Add enough oil to coat the bottom of a large skillet and set it over medium heat. When the oil is shimmering and hot, add the salmon burgers to the pan. Cook for 3 to 4 minutes, until the bottoms are golden and crispy, then flip and cook the other sides for 3 to 4 minutes more. Reduce the heat to medium-low and place a slice of cheese on top of each burger. Cover the pan with a lid to allow the steam to help melt the cheese quickly.

Smear a generous amount of mayonnaise on both sides of each toasted burger bun. Assemble the burgers by placing the patties on the bottom halves of the buns, followed by tomato slices, lettuce, red onion slices, and the bun tops.

# RAINBOW TROUT TACOS WITH PEACH AND SUNGOLD TOMATO SALSA

To no one's surprise, we've made tender smoked trout the star of this taco show. When matched with a simple peach and Sungold tomato salsa and some high-quality corn tortillas, it forms the backbone of a delicious, moderate-effort summer feast. This salsa is endlessly versatile and can be made with nectarines in place of peaches, or even with firm persimmons in place of both the peaches and Sungolds if you want to bring this feast with you into the fall. While you can certainly use any type of ripe tomato, we particularly love the mild sweetness of a Sungold. We recommend seeking them out from your local farmer's market in the height of summer.

**SERVES 4**

### FOR THE PEACH AND SUNGOLD TOMATO SALSA

2 ripe peaches, pitted and finely diced

8 ounces Sungold tomatoes, quartered

1 medium yellow onion, finely diced

4 garlic cloves, minced

2 jalapeños, 1 minced and 1 thinly sliced

Zest of 1 lime

Juice of 3 limes

¼ cup extra virgin olive oil

Fine sea salt and freshly ground black pepper

### FOR THE TACOS

12 corn tortillas

½ cup sour cream

2 or 3 tins Fishwife Smoked Rainbow Trout

1 avocado, sliced and seasoned with fine sea salt

1 handful of fresh cilantro leaves

Lime wedges, for serving

Your favorite hot sauce (optional)

**TO MAKE THE SALSA:** In a medium bowl, combine the peaches, tomatoes, onion, garlic, minced jalapeños, lime zest, lime juice, and olive oil. Mix well to combine, then season with a generous pinch of salt and a few grinds of pepper. Taste for seasoning and adjust with more salt if needed. Set aside while you prepare the rest of your mise en place. This salsa gets better with time, so feel free to make it up to a day in advance. If you have any salsa left over after your taco feast, store it in an airtight container in the fridge for up to 5 days.

**TO MAKE THE TACOS:** Heat the corn tortillas according to their package instructions and keep them warm in a clean kitchen towel. Assemble all of the other components in your favorite plates and bowls and set them out on the table.

To build a perfect taco, smear a spoonful of sour cream on a warm tortilla, layer on a couple forkfuls of smoked trout, then add a couple slices of avocado, a generous spoonful of the salsa, a few slices of jalapeño, and some cilantro leaves. Squeeze a wedge of lime juice over the top, and add a few dashes of your favorite hot sauce if you like your taco extra spicy.

# CHILI CRISP SALMON PANZANELLA

A panzanella is a stale-bread salad: Day-old bread is torn into bite-size pieces and then toasted into chewy, crunchy croutons that briefly soak up the juices of whatever else you choose to construct your salad with. Tying for first place with homemade breadcrumbs, a panzanella is one of our favorite uses for a rejected loaf of sourdough bread. The ideal level of stale is a loaf that's a day or two old, but you can make a worthy panzanella even if your forgotten loaf has turned to brick—simply pour a thin stream of water onto your hardened loaf and pop it into a preheated 350°F oven for 10 to 15 minutes; the resulting steam will nudge it back to life. This rendition leans on the convenient delight of a frozen bag of peas and a tin of our flavor-loaded chili crisp smoked salmon to create a fabulously textured summer salad.

## SERVES 2

¼ cup plus 2 tablespoons extra virgin olive oil

½ loaf stale sourdough bread, cut into bite-size pieces (about 2 heaping cups)

Fine sea salt

1 cup frozen peas

1 medium shallot, thinly sliced

3 tablespoons rice wine vinegar, plus an extra splash for seasoning the peas

1 garlic clove, grated or very finely minced

1 tablespoon finely chopped fresh parsley, plus whole sprigs for garnish

Freshly ground black pepper

1 tin Fishwife Smoked Salmon with Sichuan Chili Crisp

2 tablespoons thinly sliced scallions

In a medium bowl, pour in 2 tablespoons of the olive oil. Add the bread and a generous sprinkle of salt. Toss to coat, making sure every surface of bread is well lubricated. Heat a large, heavy-bottomed skillet over medium heat. When hot but not smoking, add the pieces of bread to the pan and spread out evenly. Cook, tossing and agitating the pan occasionally, until the bread pieces are beautifully golden on all sides. The objective is for a nice crispy exterior with a fudgy interior. Set aside to cool while you prepare the other components.

Bring a small pot of water to a boil over high heat and season generously with salt. Prepare an ice bath by adding ice cubes and water to a large bowl. Quickly blanch the peas by dropping them into the boiling water for 30 seconds. Remove the peas with a mesh sieve and immediately transfer them to the prepared ice bath.

To make the vinaigrette, add the sliced shallot to a small bowl, season with a pinch of salt, and cover with the rice wine vinegar. Set aside to macerate for 5 minutes. This softens the pungency of the raw shallot, mimicking the effect of a quick pickle. Add the garlic, chopped parsley, another pinch of salt, a generous grind of pepper, and the remaining ¼ cup of olive oil. Whisk vigorously to emulsify.

Strain the blanched and shocked peas, place them in a small bowl, and season them with a pinch of salt and a splash of rice wine vinegar.

To assemble the panzanella, place the fried bread, peas, smoked salmon, and sliced scallions in a medium bowl. Drench the mixture with the vinaigrette and toss well to combine. A panzanella does well with a moment to sop up all the juices, allowing the bread to hydrate in the flavor. Plate and garnish with a few sprigs of fresh parsley.

# DINNER IS SERVED

At the end of a long day's work, instead of defrosting the chicken, marinating the tofu, or braising the beef, we invite you to simply pop open your tinned fish of choice.

In this chapter, we'll share some of our favorite easy dinners to serve to your loved ones, from a sumptuous smoked salmon macaroni and cheese to a simple sardine pesto pasta that's sure to please even the pickiest of eaters.

# Dinner Is Served

Smoked Salmon and Caramelized Shallot Pasta with Crème Fraîche and Kale / 97

A Tuna Melt for the Whole Family / 100

Sardine and Pesto Pasta with Charred Broccolini / 103

Deep Dive: Make a Frozen Pizza Hot with Tinned Fish / 105

Fried Rice with Peas, Carrots, Scallions, and Smoked Mackerel / 106

Trout Orzo with Kale, Green Olive, and Parmesan / 109

Spaghetti Vongole with Cockles / 111

Risotto with Tinned Octopus and Smoked Paprika / 114

Smoked Salmon Mac and Cheese / 117

# SMOKED SALMON AND CARAMELIZED SHALLOT PASTA WITH CRÈME FRAÎCHE AND KALE

This weeknight pasta makes for a nutritious and delicious dinner, and can be on the table from start to finish in thirty minutes. The combination of salmon, crème fraîche, and dill are a classic flavor trio. We build on these flavors with the savory depth of caramelized shallots, the crunch of toasted walnuts, and the brightness of dry white wine. Simple tricks like blanching the kale as the pasta cooks consolidate steps, which helps achieve a more delicious meal with less effort.

**SERVES 2**

Fine sea salt

3 cups dried campanelle or other small pasta shape

1 bunch of lacinato kale, stemmed, leaves coarsely chopped, stems finely minced

2 tablespoons unsalted butter

1 tablespoon extra virgin olive oil

1 heaping cup sliced shallots, from approximately 4 large shallots

1 cup dry white wine

1 tin Fishwife Smoked Atlantic Salmon, flaked into bite-size pieces

½ cup crème fraîche

½ cup toasted walnuts, coarsely chopped

½ cup fresh dill, chopped, plus some sprigs for garnish

Zest and juice of 1 lemon

Freshly ground black pepper

Aleppo pepper

Bring a large pot of water to a boil. Once boiling, add a generous amount of salt. The water should be well seasoned but not unpalatably so. Add the pasta and cook for 2 minutes less than the package's recommended cook time; the pasta should

RECIPE CONTINUES >

be just under al dente when you remove it from the pot, as you want it to finish cooking in the sauce. Add the kale to the pasta pot 30 seconds before the pasta has finished cooking. Drain the pasta and kale, reserving ½ cup of the pasta water.

Meanwhile, heat a large skillet over medium heat. Add the butter and olive oil to the pan and heat until the butter begins to bubble. Reduce the heat to medium-low and add the shallots. Season with a small pinch of salt and cook the shallots until they are irresistibly soft and the smell wafting through your kitchen makes you hungry, about 10 minutes. Deglaze the pan with the wine, scraping up any browned bits from the bottom of the pan. Let the wine simmer and reduce by about a third, 3 to 4 minutes.

Transfer the kale and cooked pasta to the shallot pan. Ladle in the reserved ½ cup of starchy pasta water and assertively stir the contents of the pan to help the pasta's starch give body to the sauce. Cook for a couple minutes, until the pasta is al dente. Lower the heat and stir in the salmon, crème fraîche, toasted walnuts, and chopped dill. Add the lemon juice and a pinch each of black pepper and Aleppo pepper and give it all one final stir. Taste for seasoning and adjust if needed.

To serve, top each bowl with a touch of lemon zest and a couple sprigs of fresh dill.

# A TUNA MELT
# FOR THE WHOLE FAMILY

While we're largely in the business of inspiring new, unique ways to incorporate tinned fish into your cooking, we're certainly not above celebrating the classics. And what better classic to celebrate than the almighty tuna melt! This recipe leans heavily on the usual players—mayonnaise, celery, red onion, and Dijon mustard—but gets an added *oomph* of flavor from briny capers and lemon zest. This is a great sandwich to whip up as a decadent dinner for one, but it is all the more satisfying when shared with the whole family.

**SERVES 4**

3 tins Fishwife
  Albacore Tuna

½ cup mayonnaise

2 celery stalks, finely
  chopped

½ large red onion, finely
  minced

2 tablespoons Dijon
  mustard

1 tablespoon capers,
  finely chopped

Zest of 1 lemon

1 teaspoon red pepper
  flakes

Fine sea salt and freshly
  ground black pepper

8 slices white sandwich
  bread

Unsalted butter, for
  toasting the bread

4 slices Swiss cheese

Preheat the oven to 375°F.

In a medium bowl, break the tuna into small pieces with the back of a fork. Add the mayonnaise, celery, red onion, mustard, capers, lemon zest, red pepper flakes, and a small pinch each of salt and black pepper. Mix well to combine and taste for seasoning.

Butter one side of each of the bread slices, then lay 4 slices butter side down on a baking sheet—set aside the remaining slices while you build the sandwiches. Load each slice of bread with the tuna salad and top with a slice of cheese. Place the remaining 4 pieces of bread butter side up on top of the cheese to create the sandwiches.

Bake for 5 to 6 minutes, then, using a spatula and a steady hand, flip the sandwiches over to allow them to brown on the other side. Cook for 5 to 6 minutes more, until the cheese has fully melted and the bread is golden brown and crispy around the edges.

# SARDINE AND PESTO PASTA WITH CHARRED BROCCOLINI

A good pesto pasta will forever be a go-to for a quick and satisfying weeknight dinner in our home. Please feel free to reach for your favorite store-bought pesto if you're in a pinch for time; otherwise we invite you to use this recipe for making a delicious and affordable one from scratch. We opted for using toasted pumpkin seeds in lieu of the more traditional (and notoriously more expensive) pine nuts, and we use equal parts basil and parsley for a brighter, more herbaceous rendition.

We love the flavor of charred Broccolini and urge you to not forgo this step if you have the time. If, however, you're in a hurry or dreading dirtying another pan, simply chop the Broccolini and drop it into the pasta pot when your pasta clock reads two minutes till al dente. What you'll lose in the smoky depth of flavor, you'll make up for in time and dishes saved.

**SERVES 4**

### FOR THE PESTO

1 cup toasted pumpkin seeds

1 packed cup fresh parsley leaves

1 packed cup fresh basil

3 large garlic cloves, coarsely chopped

1 cup grated Parmesan cheese

1 cup extra virgin olive oil

Zest and juice of 1 lemon

½ teaspoon fine sea salt, plus more as needed

½ teaspoon freshly ground black pepper, plus more as needed

### FOR THE PASTA

Fine sea salt

1 (16-ounce) box of dried penne rigate

1 large bunch of Broccolini, cut into bite-size pieces

1 tablespoon extra virgin olive oil

2 tins Fishwife Sardines, drained and flaked into bite-size pieces

Freshly ground black pepper

**MAKE THE PESTO:** In a food processor, combine the pumpkin seeds, parsley, basil, garlic, and Parmesan

RECIPE CONTINUES >

and pulse until finely chopped. With the food processor running on the lowest setting, slowly pour in the olive oil. Add the lemon zest, lemon juice, salt, and pepper and pulse a couple more times to combine. Taste for seasoning and adjust if necessary.

**PREPARE THE PASTA:** Bring a large pot of water to a boil. Once boiling, season the water generously with salt. Cook the pasta according to the package instructions.

While the pasta is cooking, char the Broccolini. Massage the chopped Broccolini in the olive oil and ½ teaspoon of salt. Heat a large skillet over medium-high heat. When the pan is hot and just starting to smoke, add the Broccolini. Cook, undisturbed, until the bottom of the Broccolini has started to take on a nice char, 3 to 4 minutes. Toss the pan to expose the other side of the Broccolini to direct heat, then cover the pan with a tight-fitting lid. Putting a lid on the pan at this stage in the cooking process traps in enough steam to help the Broccolini cook all the way through without burning. Remove the lid after 2 minutes and test a piece of the Broccolini; if it's not fork-tender, cover the pan again and let it cook another minute or two.

In a large bowl, add the pesto, flaked sardines, and charred Broccolini. When the pasta is al dente, remove it from the pot with a spider skimmer and transfer it immediately into the bowl. Ladle in ¼ cup of cooking water from the pot, and vigorously stir to lacquer the pasta in the pesto. Season to taste with pepper.

# DEEP DIVE

## MAKE A FROZEN PIZZA HOT WITH TINNED FISH

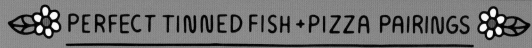 PERFECT TINNED FISH + PIZZA PAIRINGS

**FOUR-CHEESE PIZZA**
+
ANCHOVIES, ARTICHOKES, SHAVED PARM, RADICCHIO

**MARGHERITA PIZZA**
+
TUNA, KALAMATA OLIVES, FRESH BASIL

**GARLIC & PESTO PIZZA**
+
SMOKED TROUT, FRESH BASIL

**WHITE PIZZA**
+
ANCHOVIES, THYME, ONIONS

# FRIED RICE WITH PEAS, CARROTS, SCALLIONS, AND SMOKED MACKEREL

Fried rice is the best excuse to always cook more rice than needed for any given meal. The beauty of making fried rice is that chilled day-old rice is actually preferable over freshly cooked, making it the perfect dish for revamping leftovers and using up the odds and ends of any vegetables you have on hand in the fridge. Our version uses diced carrots, frozen peas, and lots of scallions, but please feel free to riff with whatever you have. Traditional fried rice often gets its umami hit from oyster sauce, but as we're clearly in the market of sneaking in tinned fish wherever it's reasonably possible, we decided to opt for the meaty, briny, umami-loaded punch of our oil-packed Cantabrian anchovies instead.

**SERVES 4**

2 tablespoons coconut oil

1 cup finely diced carrots

2 oil-packed Fishwife Cantabrian Anchovies, finely chopped

2 cups leftover cooked white rice, preferably from a long-grain variety

1 cup frozen peas, thawed

2 large eggs, thoroughly whisked

2 tins Fishwife Slow Smoked Mackerel, flaked

1 cup thinly sliced scallions

2 tablespoons soy sauce, plus more to taste

1 tablespoon toasted sesame oil

Lime wedges, for serving

In a large skillet, heat 1 tablespoon of the coconut oil over medium-high heat. When the oil is hot but not smoking, add the carrots and anchovies. Cook

RECIPE CONTINUES >

until the anchovies have melted into the oil and the carrots have barely softened, 2 to 3 minutes.

Add the rice to the pan and flatten it out evenly so that as much rice as possible is making direct contact with the bottom of the pan. Cook, undisturbed, for about 5 minutes. Using a spatula, gently peek at the bottom of the rice—it should be deeply golden and crispy. If it's not, allow it to cook for a few more minutes. Add the peas. Stir to evenly distribute everything in the pan.

Reduce the heat to medium-low and use the spatula to push the rice and veggies over to one side. Add the remaining 1 tablespoon of coconut oil to the empty space in the pan, then pour in the eggs. Gently scramble the eggs until soft curds form, then slowly reincorporate the rice and veggies.

Add the mackerel, scallions, soy sauce, and sesame oil. Stir to evenly incorporate everything and cook for another minute or two to allow the mackerel to warm through and the flavors to come to life. Taste for seasoning and adjust with more soy sauce if necessary. Serve with lime wedges.

# TROUT ORZO WITH KALE, GREEN OLIVE, AND PARMESAN

## by Sara Tane

We love how well tiny pasta shapes like orzo or couscous absorb the campfirey-ness of our trout, salmon, or mackerel, and we encourage you to swap your favorite tins of smoked fish into this recipe as you see fit. We delight in the range of textures and flavors in this dish—the crunch of the toasted almonds meeting the silkiness of the sautéed kale and orzo, the sweet smokiness of the trout elevating the briny bite of the green olive. This dish keeps well for about five days in an airtight container in the fridge, so we strongly recommend it for Sunday-night meal prepping. You can freshen it each day with a squeeze of lemon juice and a touch of grated Parmesan.

**SERVES 4 TO 6**

1½ cups dried orzo pasta

Fine sea salt

3 tablespoons extra virgin olive oil, plus more as needed

1 medium shallot, chopped

Freshly ground black pepper

4 garlic cloves, minced

⅓ cup pitted green olives, coarsely chopped

2 tins Fishwife Smoked Rainbow Trout

3 cups chopped curly kale

Zest and juice of 1 lemon

½ cup freshly grated Parmesan cheese, plus more to finish

⅓ cup toasted almonds, coarsely chopped

2 tablespoons fresh parsley, chopped

2 tablespoons unsalted butter

To prepare the orzo, bring a large pot of water to a boil. Once boiling, season the water generously with salt. Cook the orzo according to the package instructions until al dente. Drain the orzo, reserving

RECIPE CONTINUES >

1 cup of the pasta water. Toss the orzo with some olive oil to prevent it from sticking together.

In a Dutch oven, heat the 3 tablespoons olive oil over medium heat. Once shimmering, add the shallot, season with salt and pepper to taste, and cook until softened, about 4 minutes. Add the garlic and continue cooking until fragrant, about 1 minute. Add the olives and trout, and use the back of a fork or wooden spoon to gently flake the trout. Add the kale, lemon zest, and lemon juice and sauté until the kale has wilted, 2 to 3 minutes.

Stir in the orzo, Parmesan, almonds, parsley, and butter and give it a minute for everything to warm and the butter to melt. Add a splash of the reserved pasta water (you won't need it all) to make a glossy sauce. Serve on a platter with a drizzle of olive oil and more grated Parm.

# SPAGHETTI VONGOLE WITH COCKLES

*Spaghetti alle vongole,* Italian for "spaghetti with clams," is a well-loved dish consisting of little more than its title suggests. A simple pan sauce of butter, white wine, and parsley lays the foundation; the clams then release their briny liquor into the sauce, adding a nuanced seasoning that salt alone could never achieve. The long al dente noodles are the perfect vehicle to sop up all the flavor. This recipe riffs on the fundamental tenets of the classic but trades tins of cockles for fresh clams, making this already quick cooking dish come together in a breeze. The trick to maximizing the flavor of the tiny tinned shellfish in this version is adding all the juice in the tin to the sauce.

**SERVES 4**

Fine sea salt

9 ounces dried spaghetti

¼ cup extra virgin olive oil, plus more to finish

4 garlic cloves, thinly sliced

½ teaspoon red pepper flakes, plus more to finish

½ cup dry white wine

2 (4-ounce) tins cockles in brine

1 tablespoon unsalted butter

¼ cup finely chopped fresh parsley

Fresh lemon juice

Bring a large pot of water to a boil. Once boiling, season the water with a generous handful of salt. Add the spaghetti and cook according to the package instructions for 2 minutes less than its suggested cook time. Drain the pasta, reserving 1 cup of the cooking liquid.

Meanwhile, in a large skillet, heat the olive oil over medium heat. Add the garlic and red pepper flakes, swirl to coat in the oil, and cook for 1 minute. Garlic will burn in a blink, so keep a watchful eye on it and reduce the heat if it takes on color too quickly. Add the white wine to the pan. Bring it to a gentle boil, then reduce the heat to a voracious simmer. Cook for a minute or two to allow the majority of the alcohol to cook off.

Add the spaghetti to the pan along with ½ cup of the reserved cooking liquid and allow the spaghetti to simmer in the sauce until it's almost al dente—this

**RECIPE CONTINUES >**

shouldn't take much longer than a minute or two. Add the cockles and their brine and the butter. Using a wooden spoon, aggressively stir in a circular motion as though you were creating a mini vortex. This motion helps the pasta release enough starch to give body to the sauce. If the pan looks dry, add another splash of the reserved cooking liquid. When the pasta is thoroughly slicked in sauce, add the parsley and a generous squeeze of lemon juice and give everything a final toss.

Finish with a drizzle of olive oil and another pinch of red pepper flakes.

# RISOTTO WITH TINNED OCTOPUS AND SMOKED PAPRIKA

Making risotto isn't as complicated, demanding, or time-consuming as you might expect. Once you've gathered all your mise en place, a luscious, steaming bowl of risotto can be on the table in as little as thirty minutes. If there's any one tip we could give you, it's to make sure that you're using the best rice and the most delicious stock you can get your hands on. This dish will only ever be better than the sum of its parts if those parts are in and of themselves delicious.

This version is smoky, meaty, and deeply savory thanks to tinned octopus and smoked paprika.

## SERVES 4

3½ to 4 cups vegetable stock

2 tablespoons extra virgin olive oil

1 medium red onion, finely diced

Fine sea salt

2 garlic cloves, minced

1 teaspoon smoked paprika

1 teaspoon sweet paprika

1 teaspoon dried thyme

1 tablespoon tomato paste

Freshly ground black pepper

1 cup arborio or carnaroli rice

1 cup red wine

2 tablespoons unsalted butter

2 (4-ounce) tins octopus, drained

2 teaspoons sherry vinegar, plus more to taste

In a small saucepan, warm the vegetable stock over low heat.

In a medium saucepan, combine the olive oil, onion, and a small pinch of salt over medium heat. Cook until the onion is soft and translucent, about 8 minutes. Add the garlic, smoked paprika, sweet paprika,

**RECIPE CONTINUES >**

thyme, tomato paste, and a generous pinch each of salt and black pepper. Cook for 2 to 3 minutes, until everything is deeply aromatic and the tomato paste has begun to caramelize. Add the rice and stir to coat. Season with another generous pinch of salt. Deglaze the pan with the wine and bring to a simmer. Add 2 generous ladlefuls of the warm stock and return to a gentle simmer. Stir occasionally and cook until the rice has soaked up all but the smallest puddle of liquid. Add another couple ladlefuls of stock and repeat the same process (stir, simmer, stir, ladle—always making sure the rice has soaked up all but the dregs of each addition of liquid before adding more) until you're almost out of stock and the rice is just al dente. This process usually takes 20 to 25 minutes, but it depends on your rice and the temperature of the stock.

When the rice is al dente, add the butter, octopus, and sherry vinegar and stir to combine. Once the butter has melted, taste for seasoning and adjust with another pinch of salt or splash of sherry vinegar if needed. Serve topped with a grind of black pepper.

# SMOKED SALMON MAC AND CHEESE

Lobster mac and cheese is the height of decadent luxury, but we're here to propose a new, more affordable, and arguably more delicious take on the dish by opting for tins of our smoked salmon in lieu of lobster. There are a few tricks to avoiding a dry and overcooked baked mac and cheese: First, initially undercook the pasta by just a smidge, then allow it to cook fully in the hot cheesy lava; second, make sure the pasta is generously coated in more sauce than what feels acceptable; and third, trade in a longer bake time for a quick trip to the broiler—allowing a golden, blistery crust to form without risking the pasta absorbing too much of the sauce.

**SERVES 2 TO 4**

Fine sea salt

3 heaping cups dried macaroni

3 tablespoons unsalted butter

3 tablespoons all-purpose flour

3 cups whole milk

Freshly ground black pepper

4 ounces provolone cheese, grated

4 ounces Gruyère cheese, grated

4 ounces sharp white Cheddar cheese, grated

1 teaspoon Dijon mustard

1 small pinch of cayenne pepper

2 tins Fishwife Smoked Atlantic Salmon, drained

¼ cup Anchovy Sourdough Breadcrumbs (page 9, optional)

Bring a large pot of water to a boil. Once boiling, season the water with a generous handful of salt. Add the macaroni and cook according to the package instructions until just al dente. The pasta will briefly continue cooking under the broiler, so it's important not to overcook the pasta in this step.

**RECIPE CONTINUES >**

In a large saucepan, heat the butter over medium heat until fully melted and starting to bubble. Add the flour, stir to coat in the butter, and cook until it's taken on a toasty aroma and is golden in color. Add ½ cup of the milk and stir well to incorporate the roux. Add the remaining 2½ cups of milk and a generous pinch each of salt and pepper, then bring the mixture up to a gentle boil, stirring occasionally to prevent a film from forming. Reduce the heat to maintain a simmer and cook for 5 to 8 minutes, until the sauce has noticeably thickened. Don't rush this process, as you'll risk having the sauce taste like raw flour. Add all three cheeses, the mustard, and cayenne pepper. Stir to incorporate, allowing the cheese to melt. Add the cooked macaroni and smoked salmon to the pot and stir to coat all the nooks and crannies in your glorious cheese sauce.

Preheat the broiler.

Pour the mac and cheese into a 9 × 9-inch baking dish. If using the breadcrumbs, scatter them evenly on top. Place the baking dish on the top rack under your broiler and cook for 1 to 2 minutes, until the surface is covered in golden brown blisters.

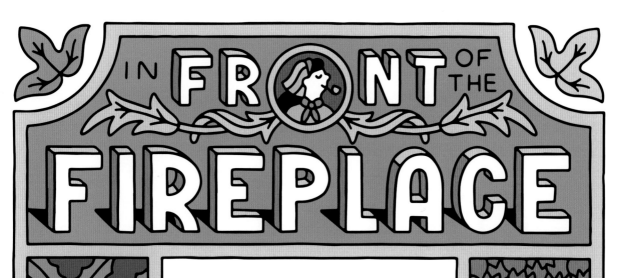

# IN FRONT OF THE FIREPLACE

As the leaves turn golden, the days grow short and chilly, and the school semester begins, there arrives Cozy Tinned Fish Season (which we believe is wildly underrated). Cozy Tinned Fish Season is full of warming congees, healing chowders, and beautiful bologneses. With more time to spend inside cooking, we've put together a handful of recipes that you can spend your Sunday afternoon in your kitchen preparing, relishing every chop, simmer, and slice.

# In Front of the Fireplace

Mushroom and Thyme Congee with Smoked Salmon / 123

Foil Dinner with Chili Crisp Salmon / 127

Lamb Bolognese with Cantabrian Anchovies / 129

Deep Dive: An Ode to Tinned Fish Chowder / 131

Spiced Mackerel Pâté with Grilled Bread / 132

Dan Dan Noodles with Smoked Salmon / 135

Smoked Mackerel Udon / 137

Smoked Salmon Chowder with Potatoes and Corn / 140

Jansson's Temptation: Potato, Cream, Onion, and Anchovy Gratin / 143

Fisherman's Stew with Salmon, Mussels, Cockles, and Saffron Aioli / 146

# MUSHROOM AND THYME CONGEE WITH SMOKED SALMON

Congee is a traditional Chinese rice porridge, cooked low and slow in a savory broth till it reaches a soft, silky, and soupy consistency. It's the perfect dish to eat when you're under the weather or when the weather itself is making you feel down. In this rendition, short-grain rice is cooked with coconut milk, mushrooms, thyme, and a velvety chicken bone broth, resulting in a dish that's just as evocative of the classic as it is of cream of mushroom soup. We serve ours topped with chili crisp salmon, lots of fresh cilantro, and lime.

**SERVES 4**

2 teaspoons coconut oil

1 small yellow onion, diced

Fine sea salt

2 heaping cups (approximately ½ pound) coarsely chopped oyster mushrooms

1 tablespoon fresh thyme leaves, lightly chopped

2 teaspoons soy sauce

1 cup short-grain white rice

1 quart chicken bone broth

1 (13.5-ounce) can full-fat coconut milk

3 garlic cloves

1 tin Fishwife Smoked Salmon with Sichuan Chili Crisp

1 handful of fresh cilantro leaves

2 limes, cut into wedges

In a medium saucepan, heat the coconut oil over medium-low heat, swirl to coat the pan, then add the onion. Stir to coat and season with a pinch of salt. Cook until translucent and aromatic, about 6 minutes.

**RECIPE CONTINUES >**

Increase the heat to medium, add the mushrooms and thyme, and stir to coat. Season with another pinch of salt and cook, stirring, for 3 to 5 minutes more. You want the mushrooms to gently brown and release some of their moisture. When they have sufficiently softened and have just barely browned, add the soy sauce. Add the rice, coating it thoroughly in the mushroom and onion mixture, and allow to cook for 1 minute more.

Add the bone broth, coconut milk, and 1 tablespoon of salt. At first glance, it will look like the rice is drowning in an impossible amount of liquid, but have faith! Rice is a thirsty grain and will surprise you with its ability to soak it all up. Bring the mixture to a gentle boil, then immediately reduce the heat to a simmer. Cook low and slow for 30 to 40 minutes, stirring every once in a while, until the congee reaches the consistency of a soupy porridge.

Serve hot, each serving topped with chili crisp salmon, cilantro, and 1 or 2 wedges of lime.

RECIPE NOTE: If you plan on making this ahead of time, make sure to have an extra splash of broth and coconut milk on hand when it's time to serve. Similar to risotto, congee will thicken significantly after sitting. Simply add enough liquid when reheating to bring it back to your desired consistency.

# FOIL DINNER
# WITH CHILI CRISP SALMON

If you've ever dated a Boy Scout (or were one yourself), you understand the immense satisfaction provided by a classic foil dinner. If you're not familiar, let us acquaint you: A foil dinner usually consists of potatoes, onions, carrots, and seasoned ground beef, all tucked snuggly into an aluminum foil envelope before being slowly grilled over a flame. It's perfect camping food, hence the ubiquitous Boy Scout tradition, but is also suitable for a cozy dinner at home. Our version opts for a couple cans of chili crisp salmon in lieu of the ground beef and features Japanese sweet potatoes and scallions for a lighter, more wholesome spin.

**SERVES 2**

2 cups diced Japanese sweet potatoes, cut into ½-inch cubes

1 bunch of scallions, cut in half horizontally

2 teaspoons coconut oil, melted

1 teaspoon fine sea salt

2 tins Fishwife Smoked Salmon with Sichuan Chili Crisp

2 tablespoons Kewpie mayonnaise, for serving (optional)

2 teaspoons toasted sesame seeds, for serving (optional)

Fresh Thai basil, for garnish (optional)

If you're cooking your foil dinner over a campfire, build that fire! If you're feeling less ambitious, preheat the oven to 375°F.

In a large bowl, combine the sweet potatoes, scallions, coconut oil, and salt and toss well to combine. Lay out two 10-inch squares of aluminum foil on your work surface. Add half of the seasoned vegetables to each piece of foil. Add 1 tin of chili crisp salmon, along with all the flavorful oil in the tin, to each foil packet. Use a fork to flake the salmon fillets into bite-size pieces and evenly distribute them with the sweet potatoes and scallions. Fold the aluminum foil over itself until you have a neat little package. If you are cooking these over a fire, it's worth double wrapping each package to prevent the loss of any flavorful juices to the flame.

If you're cooking your foil dinner over a flame, place the packets on a grate set over hot coals or embers.

**RECIPE CONTINUES >**

(Make sure to avoid placing these over a direct flame, as you risk burning both the aluminum foil and the precious cargo it's protecting.) Cook for 20 to 25 minutes, using tongs to carefully turn the packages halfway through. Test the potatoes for doneness by removing a foil packet from the grill, peeling back the foil, and piercing a piece of potato with a fork. The sweet potatoes are finished when they are soft and fudgy.

If you're cooking in the oven, place the foil packets on a baking sheet and bake for 25 to 30 minutes. There is no need to flip the packages halfway through, as there's no direct heat coming from the bottom. Remove the baking sheet from the oven and gently open a foil packet to test the potatoes for doneness. If they are not soft and yielding when pierced with a fork, bake for 5 to 10 minutes more.

This dish is delicious enjoyed just as is, straight from the foil. However, if you feel like dressing it up a bit, serve with Kewpie mayonnaise, a scattering of toasted sesame seeds, and a few leaves of Thai basil.

# LAMB BOLOGNESE
# WITH CANTABRIAN ANCHOVIES

There's little better than the comfort of hearty, rib-sticking meals in the depths of winter. This Bolognese is our go-to for the coldest days of the year, when nothing but a deeply satiating stew will do. We make our Bolognese with ground lamb, a meat celebrated for its warming nature, and lean on heady seasonings like cumin, sumac, and thyme to complement its inherently rich and grassy flavor.

The Bolognese needs hours to cook, but the bubbling cauldron doesn't require much more of your attention than an occasional stir, making it the perfect dish to cook on an evening when you'll be puttering around the house or, better yet, reading a book in front of your fireplace.

**SERVES 4**

3 tablespoons extra virgin olive oil

1 large red onion, finely diced

Fine sea salt

6 large garlic cloves, minced

4 oil-packed Fishwife Cantabrian Anchovies, finely chopped

2 tablespoons ground cumin

1 tablespoon ground sumac

1 tablespoon dried thyme

1 tablespoon Aleppo pepper or other mild, fruity ground chile

1 pound ground lamb, preferably pasture-raised

1 tablespoon capers, drained and minced

1 cup red wine

1 cup beef, lamb, or vegetable broth

1 (28-ounce) can crushed tomatoes

Fresh parsley and freshly ground black pepper, for garnish

Cooked pasta or polenta, for serving

RECIPE CONTINUES >

In a Dutch oven or other large, heavy-bottomed pot, heat the olive oil over medium-high heat. Add the diced onion and season with a small pinch of salt. Cook, stirring occasionally, for 8 to 10 minutes, until the onion has fully softened and has just started to take on a bit of color.

Add the garlic and anchovies. Cook until the garlic is aromatic and the anchovies have melted, 1 or 2 minutes more. Add the cumin, sumac, thyme, and Aleppo pepper and cook for another minute to allow the spices to bloom. Add the lamb, capers, and 2 teaspoons of salt, and stir well to coat. Add the red wine, broth, and crushed tomatoes. Bring the mixture to a gentle boil, then reduce the heat to a steady simmer. At first it will seem like an impossible amount of liquid, but have trust! If you allow time to do its job, you'll have a thick, luscious Bolognese in a matter of hours.

Cook, partially covered, for 2 to 2½ hours, until the sauce is thick and luscious. Stir occasionally to make sure nothing is sticking to the bottom of the pot. Taste for seasoning and add another generous pinch of salt if necessary.

Serve, showered in parsley and black pepper, on a bed of pasta or warm polenta.

# DEEP DIVE

## AN ODE TO TINNED FISH CHOWDER

AT FISHWIFE, WE BELIEVE THERE'S NO SUCH THING AS TOO MUCH CHOWDER. CHOWDER IS COMFORT IN A BOWL, AND WE INVITE YOU TO CHOOSE YOUR OWN CHOWDER ADVENTURE BY PICKING YOUR FAVORITE INGREDIENTS!

TINNED SALMON, TROUT, TUNA, OR CLAMS

YELLOW ONION OR SHALLOT

CELERY STALKS, FENNEL, CORN, OR CARROTS

BUTTER, COCONUT OIL, OR OLIVE OIL

VEGETABLE OR SEAFOOD STOCK

WINE, SHERRY, OR LAGER

HEAVY CREAM OR FULL-FAT COCONUT MILK

ALWAYS GARLIC

POTATOES, SWEET POTATOES, OR CELERIAC

PARSLEY, CHIVES, OR OREGANO

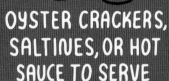

OYSTER CRACKERS, SALTINES, OR HOT SAUCE TO SERVE

# SPICED MACKEREL PÂTÉ WITH GRILLED BREAD

This spiced mackerel pâté is layered with flavor. Slowly cooked shallots add a depth of caramelized sweetness, smoked paprika intensifies the already smoky flavor of the tinned mackerel, and a touch of sherry vinegar helps to lift all the ingredients into balance. When served with thick slices of grilled bread, this pâté is a satisfying snack or light meal. We especially enjoy it in the colder months, as the fattiness of the fish and richness of the spices evoke a particular coziness.

**SERVES 2 TO 4**

2 tablespoons extra virgin olive oil, plus more for grilling the bread

2 medium shallots, minced

Fine sea salt

1 garlic clove, minced

1 teaspoon sweet red paprika

1 teaspoon smoked paprika

Freshly ground black pepper

2 tins Fishwife Slow Smoked Mackerel

1 teaspoon Calabrian chile paste, or more if you prefer a spicier pâté

1 teaspoon sherry vinegar, plus more to taste

2 to 4 slices of crusty sourdough bread

Lemon zest and freshly ground black pepper, for serving

In a small skillet, heat the olive oil over medium heat. Add the shallots and a small pinch of salt. Cook, stirring occasionally, until the shallots are caramelized and golden, 10 to 15 minutes. Reduce the heat to medium-low, then add the garlic, sweet paprika, smoked paprika, and ½ teaspoon black pepper. Cook for 2 to 3 minutes, allowing the spices to bloom and the garlic to mellow. Remove from the heat.

**RECIPE CONTINUES >**

In a food processor, combine the mackerel and the oil from the tin with the cooked shallot mixture, Calabrian chile paste, and sherry vinegar. Pulse until everything is just combined. The texture of the finished pâté should be spoonable with a few visible flakes of mackerel. We're not going for a smooth puree, so be careful not to overmix. Taste for seasoning and adjust with another pinch of salt or pepper or another splash of sherry vinegar.

Heat a grill pan over medium-high heat. Generously drizzle both sides of each slice of bread with olive oil. When the pan is very hot but not smoking, add the bread. Grill it for 3 to 4 minutes per side, until dark char marks have formed.

Serve the pâté at room temperature, garnished with lemon zest and a grind of black pepper. Enjoy slathered on the grilled bread.

# DAN DAN NOODLES WITH SMOKED SALMON

**by Sam Sujo**

This quick and easy spin on dan dan noodles allows you to achieve the particularly satisfying blend of nutty, spicy, sweet, and savory with little effort and in little time. Best of all, the recipe calls almost exclusively upon common pantry staples—smooth peanut butter, soy sauce, garlic, wheat noodles—ensuring that you can whip it up any night of the week. The precious briny oil from the bottom of our Smoked Salmon with Sichuan Chili Crisp tin adds a tingling heat to this otherwise rich and creamy dish, while the salmon itself contributes a sumptuous fattiness usually supplied by minced pork. Add steamed bok choy and chopped scallion for a balanced, deeply satisfying weeknight meal.

**SERVES 1**

### FOR THE PEANUT SAUCE

1 tablespoon creamy peanut butter

½ teaspoon sesame paste

1 garlic clove, grated

1 teaspoon soy sauce

½ teaspoon sugar

1 tin Fishwife Smoked Salmon with Sichuan Chili Crisp

### FOR THE DAN DAN NOODLES

Fine sea salt

4 ounces dried noodles of your preference (I use flat ribbon noodles, but any wheat noodle works great here)

3 baby bok choy, thoroughly rinsed

1 tablespoon chopped peanuts

1 scallion, finely chopped

**MAKE THE PEANUT SAUCE:** In a large bowl, combine the peanut butter, sesame paste, garlic, soy sauce, and sugar. Add 1 teaspoon of oil from the tin of smoked salmon. Mix to combine.

RECIPE CONTINUES >

**PREPARE THE DAN DAN NOODLES:** Bring a large pot of water to a boil and season with a generous pinch of salt. Once boiling, add the noodles and cook according to the package instructions. When there's about 2 minutes remaining on the timer, add the baby bok choy to the pot to blanch. Drain the noodles and baby bok choy. Use tongs to remove the bok choy to a plate and set aside.

Add the noodles to the sauce and thoroughly mix to combine. Mix in the salmon and any remaining oil from the tin. Top with the chopped peanuts, scallion, and baby bok choy.

# SMOKED MACKEREL UDON

Chewy udon noodles, meaty mackerel, and just-cooked greens all mingling in a steaming hot broth—also known as the most satisfying salve for winter's chill. This weeknight noodle bowl is jam-packed with flavor and comes together quickly. The beauty of the dish also lies in its versatility; feel free to substitute in any vegetables, mushrooms, or herbs you have on hand.

**SERVES 2**

Fine sea salt

8 ounces dried udon noodles

2 tablespoons sesame oil

4 garlic cloves, thinly sliced

1 tablespoon grated ginger

1 cup sliced shiitake mushrooms

2 teaspoons soy sauce, plus more to taste

1 tablespoon mirin

4 cups vegetable or chicken broth

1 small bunch of bok choy, thoroughly rinsed and cut into bite-size pieces

1 tin Fishwife Slow Smoked Mackerel, drained

Lime wedges, for serving

2 soft-boiled eggs, for serving (see Note, page 139)

Aleppo pepper

⅓ cup finely chopped scallions

Bring a large pot of water to a boil. Once boiling, season generously with salt. Add the udon noodles and cook according to the package instructions. Drain the noodles and set aside.

Meanwhile, in a medium saucepan, heat the sesame oil over medium heat. Add the garlic and ginger and cook until the garlic has softened and smells aromatic, 1 to 2 minutes. Add the mushrooms and stir to coat in the garlic and ginger mixture. Cook,

**RECIPE CONTINUES >**

undisturbed, until the mushrooms have begun to take on a bit of color, 3 to 4 minutes. Deglaze the pot with the soy sauce and mirin.

Add the broth and bring to a boil. Lower the heat to maintain a gentle simmer. Add the bok choy and simmer until tender, 3 to 4 minutes. Take the pot off the heat, add the cooked udon noodles, and flake in the mackerel fillets. Finish with a generous squeeze of lime. Taste for seasoning and adjust with another squeeze of lime or a dash of soy sauce if necessary.

Serve piping-hot, each serving topped with a halved soft-boiled egg, dusted with Aleppo pepper, and a scattering of scallions.

**RECIPE NOTE:** While we generally prefer a jammy egg for most occasions, a brothy noodle bowl warrants an especially soft-boiled egg—there's nothing like the golden yolk of an egg oozing into the hot broth, adding an invaluable richness to the dish. To soft-boil an egg, follow the technique for Perfectly Jammy Eggs (page 11), but cook for only 6 minutes.

# SMOKED SALMON CHOWDER WITH POTATOES AND CORN

This smoked salmon chowder hits all the notes of a traditional chowder (soft potatoes, a luscious creamy base, flakes of tender fish), but relies on tins of fish instead of fresh fillets. This is a particularly cozy soup to turn to on the coldest days of the year, but it also emulates the spirit of summer thanks to the convenient luxury of frozen corn. If you prefer your chowder on the thicker side, whisk in a couple tablespoons of arrowroot once you've taken the pot off the stove.

**SERVES 4**

2 tablespoons unsalted butter

½ medium yellow onion, finely diced

2 celery stalks, finely chopped

Fine sea salt

4 garlic cloves, minced

1 teaspoon dried thyme

½ teaspoon red pepper flakes

⅓ cup dry white wine

4 golf-ball-size Yukon Gold potatoes, cut into ¼-inch cubes

3 cups seafood or vegetable stock

1 cup heavy cream

Freshly ground black pepper

1 cup frozen corn kernels

2 tins Fishwife Smoked Atlantic Salmon

1 teaspoon Worcestershire sauce

2 tablespoons arrowroot powder (optional)

Chopped fresh parsley, crushed saltine crackers, and hot sauce, for serving

In a large saucepan, heat the butter over medium heat. When it's melted and bubbling, add the onion, celery, and a generous pinch of salt. Cook, stirring occasionally, until the vegetables have softened and are just starting to take on some color, about 10 minutes.

**RECIPE CONTINUES >**

Add the garlic, thyme, and red pepper flakes and cook for 1 minute more. Add the wine and simmer until its reduced by a third. Add the potatoes, seafood stock, heavy cream, and a generous pinch each of salt and black pepper. Bring the mixture to a gentle boil, then reduce the heat to maintain a steady simmer. Simmer for 15 to 20 minutes, until the potatoes are tender.

Add the frozen corn, tinned salmon, and Worcestershire sauce. Cook for another minute to allow the salmon to warm through, then remove from the heat. Taste for seasoning and adjust if needed.

If using, place the arrowroot in a small bowl and ladle in ½ cup of the liquid from the pot. Whisk until well incorporated and no lumps remain, then pour into the chowder and give everything a gentle stir to incorporate. Give it 5 minutes to thicken the chowder.

Serve hot, each serving topped with chopped parsley, a grind of black pepper, some crushed saltines, and your favorite hot sauce.

RECIPE NOTE: Arrowroot thickens this chowder without the use of a more traditional roux, helping to ensure that all our gluten-free friends can indulge in a bowl of chowder, too. If you don't have arrowroot on hand, rest assured that your chowder will still be rather tasty—just expect a slightly less luscious consistency.

# JANSSON'S TEMPTATION: POTATO, CREAM, ONION, AND ANCHOVY GRATIN

This anchovy-laced potato casserole is as ubiquitous on the Swedish Christmas table as turkey is on the American Thanksgiving table. The dish couldn't be simpler but manages to fully alchemize ordinary ingredients like potatoes, heavy cream, and onion into something extraordinary. It's packed with the type of flavor that keeps you reaching for more, largely thanks to the savory umami that our Cantabrian anchovies impart.

**SERVES 4 TO 6**

3 large russet potatoes, cut into matchsticks (aim for about ¼ inch in width)

1 large yellow onion, thinly sliced

1 tin Fishwife Cantabrian Anchovies in Extra Virgin Olive Oil, drained and broken into small pieces

Fine sea salt and freshly ground black pepper

2 cups heavy cream

½ cup Anchovy Sourdough Breadcrumbs (page 9)

Preheat the oven to 375°F.

In a large oven-safe casserole dish, evenly distribute a quarter of the potatoes across the bottom. Layer a third of the onion slices on top and then evenly distribute a third of the anchovies over the onion. Season this layer with a small pinch each of salt and pepper.

RECIPE CONTINUES >

Repeat this process two more times, layering the potatoes, onion, and anchovies with a pinch of salt and pepper. Finish by layering on the remaining quarter of the potatoes. Season with another pinch of salt and pepper, then pour over the cream. It should reach halfway up the potato mixture. Evenly scatter the breadcrumbs over the surface of the potatoes.

Bake for 45 minutes, or until the potatoes are fork-tender and the top is golden brown. Remove from the oven and let cool for at least 15 minutes before digging in.

# FISHERMAN'S STEW WITH SALMON, MUSSELS, COCKLES, AND SAFFRON AIOLI

There's nothing quite like a steaming hot bowl of fisherman's stew to conjure the image of warmer days spent engulfed in the ocean's breeze. This recipe gets its inspiration from a traditional cioppino, a tomato-and-wine-based stew filled to the brim with fresh seafood, but relies entirely on tinned seafood. We recommend pairing this flavorful stew with a generous dollop of saffron aioli and a piece (or two, or three) of garlic-rubbed olive oil fried bread.

**SERVES 4**

2 tablespoons extra virgin olive oil

1 large shallot, minced

4 garlic cloves, 3 minced and 1 left whole for the garlic bread

½ teaspoon dried oregano

1 tablespoon fresh thyme leaves

½ teaspoon crushed red pepper flakes

¾ cup white wine

2 cups crushed tomatoes

4 cups fish stock

1 bay leaf

Fine sea salt and freshly ground black pepper

1 tin Fishwife Smoked Atlantic Salmon, drained

1 (4-ounce) tin mussels, drained

1 (4-ounce) tin cockles, drained

15 to 20 saffron threads

1 scant cup Aioli (page 3)

4 slices Olive Oil Fried Bread (page 4)

2 tablespoons chopped fresh parsley, for garnish

In a large saucepan, heat the olive oil and shallot over medium heat. Cook, stirring occasionally, until the shallot has softened, 3 to 4 minutes. Add the minced garlic, oregano, thyme, and red pepper flakes. Stir to combine and cook for 2 minutes more.

Add the wine and bring it to a simmer. Simmer for 5 minutes, or until the wine has reduced by about a third. Add the crushed tomatoes, fish stock, bay leaf, 1 teaspoon sea salt, and a generous grind of black pepper. Bring this to a boil, then reduce the heat to a gentle simmer and cook for 15 minutes. Add the salmon, mussels, and cockles and cook for 1 minute more to allow the seafood to warm through.

To make the saffron aioli, bloom the saffron threads in 1 teaspoon of warm water in a small bowl. Set it aside for 10 minutes to let the flavor extract. Pour the bloomed threads along with the water into a batch of aioli and mix well to combine.

Cut the reserved garlic clove in half and rub it on all sides of the still-warm olive oil fried bread.

Serve the stew piping hot, each serving topped with a dollop of saffron aioli and a sprinkle of chopped parsley, and enjoy with a piece of warm garlic bread.

# HOSTING A

Picture this: You show up to a cocktail party with a handful of tinned fish, a fresh baguette, cultured butter, and a tin of flaky sea salt. You lay out a serving board, crack open tins of gleaming smoked salmon, plump Cantabrian anchovies, and silvery sardines. You tear the baguette into hearty bites, schmear creamy butter—go rogue!—directly onto the board, and compose the most elegant conservas board any partygoer has ever seen. You'll be the talk of the town, and your tinned fish display will steal the night.

# COCKTAIL PARTY

# Hosting a Cocktail Party

Anchovy and Olive Martini / 151

Crispy Sunchokes with Rainbow Trout Jerky Gems / 154

Deep Dive: The Great Tinned Fish Beverage Companion Guide / 156

Anchovy Bagna Càuda with Vegetable Crudité / 157

Garlic and Lemon Marinated Anchovies and Castelvetrano Olives / 158

Tinned Smoked Salmon Deviled Eggs / 161

Tinned Mussel Escabeche / 163

Salmon with Lemon Crème Fraîche / 164

Sardine Fritto Misto with Charred Lemon and Aioli / 165

Caramelized Onion and Anchovy Tart / 168

# ANCHOVY AND OLIVE MARTINI

A cocktail party isn't a cocktail party without a good cocktail, and what better cocktail to accompany a feast of tinned fish–inspired bites than an ice-cold martini adorned with a booze-soaked anchovy and a briny olive? We turned to Kevin King, a dear friend of Fishwife and a truly masterful bartender (who among other notable achievements, has designed and developed impressive bar programs for many of the Neighborhood Dining Group's restaurants, including—but not limited to—Husk Savannah, Delaney Oyster House, and Minero John's Island), to develop a unique but approachable technique for utilizing a tin of anchovies, oil and all, to enhance a classic martini. This is what he came up with: a clean, savory rendition that infuses your chosen spirit (vodka or gin) with the unctuous oil left over in the anchovy tin.

This recipe for the infused spirit and brined anchovies yields enough to make 8 martinis. Note that the measurements in the instructions for the martini are for mixing one drink; we encourage you to scale up the recipe according to how many guests you're serving.

## ALCOHOL-BRINED ANCHOVIES AND ANCHOVY OLIVE OIL–INFUSED ALCOHOL

**MAKES ENOUGH FOR 8 COCKTAILS**

1 (750 ml) bottle of vodka or gin
1 tin Fishwife Cantabrian Anchovies in Extra Virgin Olive Oil

**MAKE THE ALCOHOL-BRINED ANCHOVIES:** Grab your favorite bottle of vodka or gin. Use a shot glass to measure out 2 ounces and place the liquor into a small jar. Carefully open one tin of Cantabrian anchovies, making sure to leave all the oil in the tin. Add the anchovies to your jar to brine in the alcohol for at least 1 hour and set aside for martini time later. These booze-brined anchovies will keep in an airtight container in the fridge for up to 1 week.

RECIPE CONTINUES >

**MAKE THE INFUSED ALCOHOL:** Funnel the olive oil from the tin into the bottle of liquor. Cap and shake the bottle, then let it rest for at least 1 hour. After infusing, place the bottle in the freezer overnight. The next day, pull the bottle from the freezer and strain the entire contents through a coffee filter to catch the solidified olive oil. Return the strained, infused spirit to the bottle and discard the olive oil. If kept in the freezer, the infused spirit will keep indefinitely—but for the freshest flavor, we recommend consuming within 2 weeks.

## ANCHOVY AND OLIVE MARTINI

**SERVES 1**

½ ounce Spanish dry vermouth

3 ounces Anchovy Olive Oil–Infused Alcohol (recipe precedes)

1 or 2 pitted Castelvetrano olives

1 Alcohol-Brined Anchovy (recipe precedes)

Place your favorite martini glass in the freezer.

Pour the vermouth and infused alcohol into a cocktail shaker or large glass. Add a handful of ice and shake or stir until chilled and properly diluted. The best way to determine if your drink is properly chilled and diluted is to taste it: the sharp edge of the alcohol should feel a bit softer, and the chilled booze should ultimately taste like a delicious martini.

Strain the martini into the chilled martini glass. Garnish with the olive and a brined anchovy.

# CRISPY SUNCHOKES WITH RAINBOW TROUT JERKY GEMS

Every time early winter rolls around, our farmer's market brims with sunchokes. If you're not familiar with these earthy tubers, imagine the flavor as a cross between a starchy potato, a nutty chestnut, and a fresh artichoke. In this recipe, they're essentially prepared like potatoes: parboiled in salted water till just tender, then smashed and doused in olive oil before being roasted until gloriously golden brown with a soft, fudgy interior and an irresistibly crispy exterior. Top 'em with a dollop of crème fraîche, some smoky tinned trout, and a touch of dill and devour in the company of friends aplenty!

**SERVES 4 AS A SNACK**

1 pound medium
   sunchokes,
   scrubbed well

1 bay leaf

Fine sea salt to season

¼ cup extra virgin
   olive oil

¼ cup crème fraîche

1 tin Fishwife Smoked
   Rainbow Trout

Lemon zest, for garnish

Dill sprigs, for garnish

Preheat the oven to 450°F. Line a baking sheet with parchment paper.

In a small pot, combine the sunchokes, bay leaf, and a generous amount of salt (think the saltiness of pasta water). Add enough water to cover the sunchokes by an inch and bring to a boil over high heat. Cook until the sunchokes are just al dente, but no longer, 10 to 15 minutes. When the sunchokes are cooked through, drain them and set aside to cool.

Once cooled, gently smash the sunchokes, either with the bottom of a glass on a cutting board or in between the palms of your hands. Lay the smashed sunchokes out on the prepared baking sheet, generously drizzle them with the olive oil, and season with another sprinkle of salt. Bake until they are golden and crispy around the edges; depending on the size of your sunchokes, this will take between 15 and 25 minutes.

When the sunchokes are sufficiently crispy, remove them from the oven to cool. You'll want to serve them warm, but not hot, or else the crème fraîche will melt on contact. Once they've cooled down a little, dollop a spoonful of crème fraîche on each sunchoke, then top it with a small piece of trout and garnish it with a bit of lemon zest and a sprig of dill.

# DEEP DIVE
## THE GREAT TINNED FISH BEVERAGE COMPANION GUIDE

STIR UP OUR FAVORITE TINNED FISH & BEVVIE PAIRINGS.

Cantabrian Anchovies with a Wet Martini

Smoked Salmon with Lager

Sardines with Vinho Verde

Octopus with Red Wine

Tuna in Olive Oil with Sweet Red Vermouth and Olives

Mussels Escabeche with Champagne

Smoked Trout with Cider

# ANCHOVY BAGNA CÀUDA WITH VEGETABLE CRUDITÉ

*Bagna càuda*, which roughly translates to "hot bath," is a dipping sauce that's ubiquitous in the Piedmont region of Northern Italy. It consists primarily of anchovies, garlic, and olive oil. Consider it the tinned fish equivalent of fondue; the dip is served warm and plentifully, awaiting fresh or cooked vegetables to take a leisurely dunk. We've added crushed, toasted walnuts to our version for an added dimension of flavor and texture, and a touch of preserved lemon paste for a savory brightness. Both are optional, but including them makes for a particularly delicious rendition.

**SERVES 4 TO 6**

1 tin Fishwife Cantabrian Anchovies in Extra Virgin Olive Oil, finely chopped and oil reserved

4 garlic cloves, finely grated

¾ cup extra virgin olive oil

¼ cup toasted walnuts, finely chopped or crushed in a mortar and pestle (optional)

1 teaspoon preserved lemon paste (optional)

Zest of 1 lemon, plus 1 tablespoon fresh lemon juice

Freshly ground black pepper

Seasonal vegetables, for dipping

In your smallest saucepan, combine the chopped anchovies, the reserved oil from the tin, the garlic, and olive oil. Heat over low heat and cook until the anchovies have melted and the garlic is no longer raw, about 5 minutes. Fold in the walnuts and preserved lemon paste, if using, along with the lemon zest, lemon juice, and a generous grind of black pepper.

Serve the bagna càuda warm, alongside your favorite seasonal vegetables—endive, radicchio, and sweet winter carrots are some personal favorites.

# GARLIC AND LEMON MARINATED ANCHOVIES AND CASTELVETRANO OLIVES

When all else fails, a good old marinated olive will always be a reliable, welcome snack. We've added anchovies to our recipe because in our heart of hearts, more will always be more. The trick to ensuring that the anchovies retain the integrity of their shape is letting the marinated olives cool down till they're just warm before adding the anchovies to the mix. These marinated olives are equally delicious served warm or at room temperature.

**SERVES 4 TO 6**

¾ cup extra virgin olive oil

2 large garlic cloves, finely grated

Zest of 2 lemons

4 fresh thyme sprigs

1 bay leaf

1 teaspoon fennel seeds (optional)

½ teaspoon black pepper

1 cup Castelvetrano olives

1 tin Fishwife Cantabrian Anchovies in Extra Virgin Olive Oil

In a small saucepan, combine the olive oil, garlic, lemon zest, thyme, bay leaf, fennel seeds, and pepper. Cook over the gentlest heat for 10 minutes to allow the flavors to bloom. Add the olives and cook for another 5 minutes, or until the olives are thoroughly warmed through.

Remove from the heat and set aside to cool for 10 to 15 minutes, until the oil reaches a temperature you'd feel comfortable taking a long soak in. Add the anchovies to the mix, and gently stir to distribute them. Serve immediately, or store in an airtight container in the fridge for up to a week.

# TINNED SMOKED SALMON DEVILED EGGS

While we strongly believe the classic deviled egg is a near-perfect food, we challenge you to take it up a notch the next time you make them, by incorporating tinned smoked salmon and a hit of horseradish.

**SERVES 6 TO 8**

12 large eggs, at room temperature

2 tins Fishwife Smoked Atlantic Salmon

½ cup mayonnaise

2 tablespoons Dijon mustard

2 tablespoons chopped fresh chives

1 tablespoon finely chopped fresh dill, plus 1 small handful of sprigs for garnish

2 teaspoons prepared horseradish

2 teaspoons fresh lemon juice

Fine sea salt and freshly ground black pepper

Aleppo pepper

Bring a large pot of water to a boil over high heat. Once boiling, reduce the heat just a smidge to maintain a gentle boil.

Gently lower the eggs into the boiling water and immediately cover the pot with a lid. While the eggs are cooking, prepare an ice bath by filling a large bowl with ice and cold water. Boil the eggs for 9½ minutes, then remove from the heat and use a slotted spoon to transfer them to the ice bath.

Peel and halve the eggs. Gently remove the yolks and set the whites aside for later. In a large bowl, mash together the cooked yolks and salmon with the back of a fork until the mixture resembles a rough puree. Fold in the mayonnaise, mustard, chives, chopped dill, horseradish, lemon juice, and a generous pinch each of salt and pepper. Mix well until everything is evenly incorporated. Taste for seasoning and adjust if needed.

Transfer the mixture to a piping bag, then pipe out about a tablespoon's worth into each cooked egg white half. Garnish each deviled egg with a sprig of dill, a grind of black pepper, and a pinch of Aleppo pepper to finish.

# TINNED MUSSEL ESCABECHE

The word *escabeche* is an umbrella term for several meat, fish, or vegetable dishes that have been marinated in an acidic, spice-laden vinegar-and-oil brine. Many cultures, spanning from Latin America to Portugal and Spain to the Philippines, have their own relationship to and rendition of escabeche. In our version, we've let tinned mussels take center stage. When served with corn tortilla chips, this flavor-packed snack is guaranteed to satisfy.

**SERVES 4 TO 6**

⅓ cup extra virgin olive oil

½ large red onion, sliced

Fine sea salt

1 large carrot, julienned

4 large garlic cloves, thinly sliced

Freshly ground black pepper

1 teaspoon fresh thyme leaves

½ teaspoon smoked paprika

½ teaspoon red pepper flakes

⅓ cup red wine vinegar

1 teaspoon sugar

2 (4-ounce) tins mussels

Corn tortilla chips, for serving

In a small saucepan, heat the olive oil over medium-high heat. When the oil is quite hot but not smoking, add the onion slices and a small pinch of salt. Cook, stirring the onion occasionally, for 3 to 5 minutes, until it's just starting to soften and begins to take on the tiniest touch of color.

Add the julienned carrot and toss to coat. Cook for 1 to 2 minutes more, then add the sliced garlic. Season all the vegetables with ½ teaspoon each of salt and black pepper and cook for another minute or two, being careful not to let the garlic burn. Add the thyme, smoked paprika, and red pepper flakes. Take the pan off the heat, then add the vinegar and sugar. Add the mussels and give everything a good stir to combine.

Transfer the escabeche to an airtight container and marinate for at least 2 hours in the fridge. It's delicious served warm or at room temperature, but we advise against serving it straight from the fridge. If you're serving it warm, simply reheat in a saucepan set over medium-low heat until fully warmed through.

Serve with corn tortilla chips aplenty.

While we highly doubt you'll have leftovers, this escabeche will keep for up to 3 days stored in an airtight container in the fridge.

# SALMON WITH LEMON CRÈME FRAÎCHE

**by Sara Tane**

This is the ultimate low-effort, high-reward appetizer. Grab your favorite bag of potato chips and get to prepping a platterful of perfect bites for your guests by topping individual chips with a small dollop of lemony crème fraîche, a bite of salmon, green flecks of chives, and a drizzle of extra virgin olive oil. Serve at your next cocktail party and watch eyes pop and jaws drop.

**SERVES 2 TO 4**

¼ cup crème fraîche
  or sour cream

Zest of 1 lemon

Fine sea salt and freshly
  ground black pepper

24 kettle-cooked
  or ridged potato chips

1 tin Fishwife Smoked
  Atlantic Salmon, flaked
  into ½-inch pieces

Fresh chives, thinly
  sliced, for garnish

Extra virgin olive oil,
  for garnish

In a small bowl, mix together the crème fraîche and lemon zest. Season to taste with salt and pepper.

Arrange the potato chips on a serving platter. Top each chip with about 1 teaspoon of the crème fraîche mixture. Top each with a piece of salmon. Garnish with fresh chives, pepper, and olive oil and serve immediately.

# SARDINE FRITTO MISTO WITH CHARRED LEMON AND AIOLI

A quick dredge in a light rice batter transforms an ordinary tin of sardines into something sublime. These fried sardines are warm, crispy, and the perfect excuse to eat way too much aioli. Feel free to add any other types of tinned fish or vegetables, such as onions, zucchini, or fennel, or even thin slices of lemon, to the batter for a proper fritto misto feast. Charring lemons is a simple trick for concentrating the sweetness in their juice, providing for a more complex and caramelized flavor.

**SERVES 4 TO 6**

Grapeseed oil, for frying

2 lemons, halved

1¼ cups white rice flour

1 teaspoon fine sea salt

1 teaspoon baking powder

⅔ cup dry white wine

⅔ cup filtered water

3 tins Fishwife Sardines, drained

Flaky sea salt

1 scant cup Aioli (page 3), for serving

Heat a small, heavy-bottomed skillet over medium-high heat. Add a small drizzle of grapeseed oil. Place the halved lemons, cut side down, on the hot pan. Cook, undisturbed, until the cut sides have taken on a deep caramelized char, about 5 minutes. Remove from the heat and set aside.

In a large bowl, sift the rice flour and whisk in the salt, baking powder, wine, and water until a smooth, pourable batter forms.

In a medium saucepan, heat 2 inches of grapeseed oil over medium heat until it reaches 375°F. A kitchen thermometer is particularly useful for this task, but if you don't have one, you can easily gauge the heat of the oil with your naked eye: the oil will be ready when the surface has gentle ripples in it, like the gentlest ocean wave. You can also test to make sure the oil is hot enough by sliding in one batter-dredged sardine; the oil should engulf the little fishie in a sea of tiny bubbles.

RECIPE CONTINUES >

Line a baking sheet or large plate with paper towels.

One by one, dredge each sardine in the batter and gently drop it into the hot oil. Fry until golden and crispy, about 3 minutes. Remove from the oil with a spider skimmer or tongs and drain on the paper towels. Season with a pinch of flaky sea salt.

Serve the fried sardines on a large platter with the charred lemons and aioli on the side.

# CARAMELIZED ONION AND ANCHOVY TART

Unlike the majority of the recipes in this chapter, this caramelized onion and anchovy tart, more classically known as a pissaladière, begs you to take your time. First, butter and flour combine to make a flaky crust, then onions are slowly caramelized over the course of an hour. Once you have these components at the ready, you'll assemble your precious tart by topping the rolled-out buttery crust with the caramelized onions, a cross-hatching of anchovies, and a salty olive for each bite. While we certainly understand the luxury of a recipe that comes together quickly, there's a particular magic to watching the fruits of your labor bloom after a long, leisurely day in the kitchen.

**SERVES 6**

2 cups all-purpose flour, plus more for dusting

½ teaspoon sea salt, plus more to season

¾ cup (1½ sticks) cold unsalted butter, cut into small cubes

2 to 4 tablespoons ice-cold water

¼ cup extra virgin olive oil

4 large red onions, thinly sliced

1 tin Fishwife Cantabrian Anchovies in Extra Virgin Olive Oil

½ cup niçoise olives (or another assertively flavored black olive), pitted

1 large egg, whisked

A Simple Green Salad (page 10), for serving (optional)

In a food processor, briefly pulse the flour and salt to combine. Add the cubed butter and pulse 8 to 10 times, until the largest pieces of butter are no larger than a pea and no smaller than a lentil. You want the texture of the mixture to look a bit pebbly

**RECIPE CONTINUES >**

at this point. Slowly dribble in the ice-cold water as you pulse 5 to 8 times more. (This technique allows the water droplets to hit the moving blade, which helps to evenly distribute the water into the flour.) At this stage, the dough should look like hydrated pebbles—it won't look cohesive but should hold together when you squeeze a pinch of it between your fingers. The tenderness and flakiness of your crust depend on you not overworking the dough, so be careful not to overmix at this stage.

Fold the crumbly dough out onto a large piece of plastic wrap. Fold the plastic wrap over the dough like you're wrapping a present, then gently press down on the dough to help it form a cohesive mass. Place in the refrigerator to rest for at least 2 hours.

While the dough is resting, caramelize your onions. Place two large skillets over medium-low heat and distribute the olive oil evenly in each pan. Divvy out half of the onions for each pan, and season both with a generous pinch of salt. Cook, stirring occasionally, until the onions are meltingly soft and deeply caramelized. This process can take upward of an hour and shouldn't be rushed.

Preheat the oven to 425°F.

Remove the dough from the fridge 15 to 20 minutes before you plan to roll it out; you want the dough to be chilled to the touch when you begin, but you also want to give the butter enough time to briefly temper, as this will help prevent the dough from cracking as you work.

Lay a piece of parchment paper out on your work surface. Generously flour the parchment paper and both sides of the pie dough. Place the round of dough on the parchment paper, then use a rolling pin to roll the dough out into a large rectangle, approximately 14 × 10 inches. The dough should be no thicker than ⅛ inch when it's fully rolled out. Carefully transfer the parchment paper with the dough to a baking sheet.

Sprinkle a thin and even layer of flour on the rolled-out dough; this will act as a barrier from the wetness of the caramelized onions to help protect the crust from becoming soggy. Cover all but the outer inch of the rectangle with an even layer of caramelized onions. Lay the anchovies on the caramelized onions in rows, then crosshatch them by laying more rows on top in the opposite direction. Nestle an olive into each diamond-shaped space.

Gently fold over the edges of the dough. Seal the corners by pressing the dough onto itself. Brush the crust with the whisked egg; this will help give it a marvelously golden sheen.

Transfer the baking sheet to the oven and bake for about 1 hour, rotating the pan halfway through, until the crust is golden brown. Remove from the oven and let cool for 20 minutes before slicing and serving.

# LATE NIGHT

This is the chapter where we satisfy your wildest tinned fish cravings, the lip-smacking late-night wonders you've never before dared to dream of. This is the chapter of crispy grilled cheeses and nachos, of the briniest tinned fish tapenade, of the most craveable salmon and rice bowl. Dare to indulge in these delights and you'll have a night to remember.

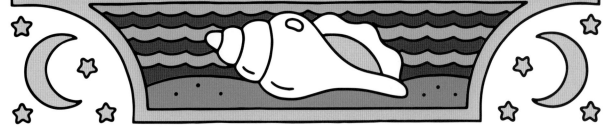

# Late Night

Grilled Cheese with Pesto and Anchovies / 175

Pantry Pasta with Chickpeas, Capers, Anchovies, and Breadcrumbs / 179

Deep Dive: Tinned Fish and Potato Chips / 181

Supreme Tinned Fish Nachos / 183

Maple-Glazed Chili Crisp Salmon with Steamed Rice and Scallions / 184

Toast with Sardine Tapenade / 187

# GRILLED CHEESE WITH PESTO AND ANCHOVIES

Once in a blue moon, a voice from beyond whispers a life-altering idea into your ear. In this case, that idea was to make anchovies the star of a grilled cheese sandwich. Anchovies bring the briny, deeply savory quality that any good, aged cheese would, and ooey-gooey mozzarella is the perfect mild and meltable counterbalance. Put them together, add a generous swipe of pesto, and you've got the most spectacular grilled cheese that you never knew you needed.

This is a perfect sandwich to feed your craving for a plump, briny anchovy at any time of day. For the sake of ease, we reached for store-bought pesto in lieu of homemade. If you're feeling ambitious and want to embark on a more time-intensive version of this grilled cheese, give our pesto recipe (see page 103) a go!

**SERVES 1**

2 slices sourdough bread

2 to 3 tablespoons pesto, homemade (see page 103) or store-bought

½ cup grated mozzarella cheese

4 oil-packed Fishwife Cantabrian Anchovies, oil reserved

Lemon zest

Freshly ground black pepper

Generously slather one side of each slice of bread in pesto. Add a thick layer of grated mozzarella cheese to one of the slices, on top of the pesto. Top the grated cheese with the anchovies and shower with a good bit of lemon zest and a generous grind of black pepper. Now layer the other slice of bread on top, pesto side down, securing all the cheesy goodness between them. Brush the top of the sandwich with half of the olive oil left in the anchovy tin.

Set a small skillet over medium heat. When the pan is hot but not smoking, carefully flip the sandwich into the pan, oiled side down. A small steak weight is great for weighing down the sandwich to help nudge along the melting of the cheese. If you don't have a steak weight, simply placing

**RECIPE CONTINUES >**

a lid over the pan can help create enough steam to melt the cheese before the bread burns; this is an especially useful trick if you're using thick-cut slices of sourdough. When the bottom side of the sandwich is sufficiently golden, about 5 minutes, brush the top with the remaining oil from the tin. Flip the sandwich and cook on the other side. The sandwich is done when both sides are golden brown and the cheese is irresistibly gooey.

# PANTRY PASTA WITH CHICKPEAS, CAPERS, ANCHOVIES, AND BREADCRUMBS

A well-stocked pantry is eternally giving when it comes to whipping up a low-effort, high-reward late-night meal. The formula for a good pantry pasta dish is forgiving but requires a few fundamentals: pasta (of course), something salty (capers, anchovies), and an allium to caramelize and add savory depth (garlic, onion, shallots). Choice extra-credit ingredients are a wilting vegetable from your fridge, cooked beans or other legumes, a handful of fresh herbs, whatever nub of grateable cheese you have around, and/or some breadcrumbs to add a welcome crunch.

In this rendition, the only fresh produce called for is parsley, which in a pinch is certainly optional.

**SERVES 2**

Fine sea salt

3 cups dried pasta, such as rigatoni or penne rigate

3 tablespoons extra virgin olive oil

2 medium shallots, thinly sliced

2 tins Fishwife Cantabrian Anchovies in Extra Virgin Olive Oil

1 tablespoon capers, coarsely chopped

2 garlic cloves, thinly sliced

½ cup cooked or canned chickpeas, drained

¼ cup fresh parsley (from 1 large handful), stemmed and coarsely chopped

¼ cup Anchovy Sourdough Breadcrumbs (page 9)

1 generous pinch of red pepper flakes

Freshly ground black pepper

Bring a large pot of water to a boil over high heat. Once boiling, add a generous amount of salt. The water should be well seasoned but not unpalatably

**RECIPE CONTINUES >**

so. Cook the pasta according to the package instructions until it's just under al dente. Drain the pasta, reserving 2 cups of the pasta water.

Heat a large skillet over medium heat. Pour in the olive oil and swirl to coat the pan. Add the shallots, stir to coat evenly in the oil, and season with a small pinch of salt. (Seasoning as you go is essential for building depth of flavor, but make sure to use a light hand, as this dish is already loaded with the saltiness of capers and anchovies.) Cook the shallots until they have softened and have taken on some color, 10 to 12 minutes—you want them to be deeply golden. Stir occasionally to prevent them from burning.

Reduce the heat to medium-low and add the anchovies. The anchovies should start to melt upon contact with the hot oil but might need a little help fully dissolving—simply smoosh them with the back of a wooden spoon until they've become one with the oil. Add the capers and garlic and cook for 2 to 3 minutes more, being careful not to let the garlic take on too much color. Add a ladleful of pasta water to the pan to create a sauce.

Increase the heat back to medium, add the chickpeas, the cooked pasta, and another ladle or two of the pasta water to the pan. Toss and stir vigorously so the pasta releases some of its starches into the sauce. Cook for another minute or two, to let the flavors meld and to allow the pasta to cook until al dente. Add the parsley and give it one final toss.

Plate and top with a generous handful of breadcrumbs, season with the red pepper flakes, and add salt and black pepper to taste.

# DEEP DIVE
## TINNED FISH AND POTATO CHIPS

DUNKING A CHIP INTO AN HERBY, CREAMY SMOKED FISH DIP IS ONE OF LIFE'S GREATEST PLEASURES. HERE'S A RUNDOWN ON HOW TO THROW TOGETHER A QUICK, PERFECT CHIPS + TINNED FISH DIP.

**SOMETHING CREAMY/FATTY**
CREAM CHEESE, SOUR CREAM, CRÈME FRAÎCHE

**A BEAUTIFUL BOWL OF POTATO CHIPS**

**SMOKED FISH**
SMOKED SALMON, SMOKED MACKEREL, SMOKED TROUT

**CHERRY ON TOP**
CAVIAR OR SMOKED TROUT ROE

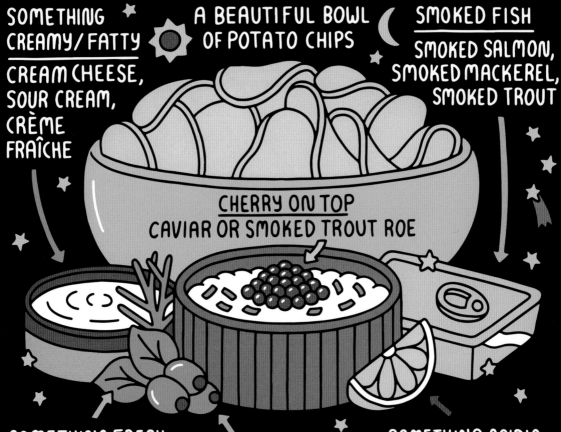

**SOMETHING FRESH**
DILL, PARSLEY, CHIVES, BASIL, RED ONIONS, SCALLIONS

**SOMETHING BRINY**
CAPERS, OLIVES

**SOMETHING ACIDIC**
LEMON JUICE, LEMON ZEST, LIME ZEST

# SUPREME TINNED FISH NACHOS

We understand if the initial thought of a tinned fish nacho feels off, but hear us out: Nachos are usually loaded up with something tender and meaty, be it pulled pork or roasted chicken. Tinned tuna is both of those things, so why wouldn't it work just as well? We're here to confirm that it is, in fact, just as delicious, if not even more so, than the aforementioned alternatives.

Turn to these nachos when you have a late-night hankering for something sloppy and satisfying, when you have friends over for an impromptu midnight feast, or when you've had one too many drinks and need something fatty, salty, and satiating that requires minimum effort.

The key to success with any nachos is making sure there's an even distribution of toppings for each chip. We achieve this by spreading the chips out in a thin, even layer on a baking sheet before loading on the goodness.

**SERVES 2 TO 4**

4 cups sturdy corn tortilla chips

2 tins Fishwife Albacore Tuna, flaked into bite-size pieces

½ cup cooked or canned black beans, drained

⅓ cup sliced black olives

½ cup shredded Monterey Jack cheese

¼ cup pickled jalapeño slices

¼ cup sour cream

⅓ cup finely chopped scallions

1 small handful of fresh cilantro leaves (optional)

Preheat the broiler.

Spread the corn tortilla chips out in an even layer on a baking sheet. Evenly distribute the pieces of tuna, beans, and olives on top. Sprinkle the cheese all over.

Broil for 2 to 5 minutes, until the cheese has melted and is starting to caramelize. Keep a close eye on the nachos, as they'll go from meltingly delicious to burnt in a blink.

Top with the pickled jalapeño, dollops of the sour cream, a scattering of the chopped scallions, and the cilantro leaves, if desired.

# MAPLE-GLAZED CHILI CRISP SALMON WITH STEAMED RICE AND SCALLIONS

There's little more comforting than coming home to the perfume of warm steamed rice after a long day's work. A rice cooker, while not a necessary kitchen appliance, brings this comfort to life effortlessly. If you don't have a rice cooker, a steamed bowl of rice is still only 30 minutes away with a small pot and a stovetop. When adorned with this simple maple-glazed chili crisp salmon and scallions, a bowl of rice transforms into a satiating, cozy late-night meal.

**SERVES 1**

1 tin Fishwife Smoked Salmon with Sichuan Chili Crisp

2 teaspoons pure maple syrup

1 cup Steamed Rice (page 8)

¼ cup thinly sliced scallions, for garnish

Toasted sesame seeds, for garnish (optional)

Place a small pan over medium-high heat. When the pan is hot but not smoking, add the entire contents from the chili crisp salmon tin and the maple syrup. Cook until the salmon is warmed through and the maple syrup has begun to caramelize, 1 to 2 minutes.

Serve the maple-glazed salmon on the steamed rice and garnish with the chopped scallions and sesame seeds, if using.

# TOAST WITH SARDINE TAPENADE

Toast with tapenade is an easy, flavor-packed snack, but it isn't particularly filling unless you eat piece of toast after piece of toast. Add a tin of sardines to the tapenade and that predicament is quickly solved—the sardines provide enough protein and essential fatty acids to transform the olive-and-garlic-laden condiment into a more substantial and nutritious dish.

Tapenade benefits from resting for a few hours before digging in, as it gives all the flavors a chance to meld and mellow into one another. If you have the time and forethought to make this ahead, please do! It keeps well in an airtight container in the fridge for up to a week; just bring it up to room temperature before enjoying.

**SERVES 2**

¼ cup pitted kalamata olives

¼ cup pitted Castelvetrano olives

1 tin Fishwife Sardines, drained

3 garlic cloves, minced

2 teaspoons extra virgin olive oil

½ teaspoon dried oregano

½ teaspoon red pepper flakes

½ teaspoon freshly ground black pepper

1 teaspoon red wine vinegar, plus more to taste

Fine sea salt

2 slices Olive Oil Fried Bread (page 4)

A few fresh parsley sprigs, for serving

Add both types of olives, the sardines, and garlic to a food processor and pulse until broken down into small pea-size pieces. Add the olive oil, oregano, red pepper flakes, black pepper, and vinegar. Pulse to combine, then taste for seasoning. Adjust with a pinch of salt or another splash of vinegar if needed.

Smear the tapenade on the fried bread and top with the sprigs of parsley.

We close the book on a misty Sunday morning, when you've got slow hours to enjoy the cooking process, you have a wild night to overcome, or you're looking to soothe your mind for the busy week ahead. These recipes—from a simple tinned fish smörgåsbord to the more involved latkes with sour cream, chives, and mackerel— are an answer to all of the above. Get the coffee brewing and enjoy.

# Sunday Morning

Tinned Fish Smörgåsbord / 191

Potato, Caramelized Onion, and Trout Hash with Herbed Yogurt / 192

Savory Miso Oats with Chili Crisp Salmon / 194

Oeufs Mayo / 197

Deep Dive: The Art of the Toast / 198

Latkes with Sour Cream, Chives, and Smoked Mackerel / 199

Smoked Salmon Frittata with Feta Cheese and Dill / 202

Chili Crisp Salmon Benedict / 205

# TINNED FISH SMÖRGÅSBORD

The word *smörgåsbord* roughly translates to "sandwich table," which is quite the fitting title for the lavish spread of breads, cheeses, cured fish, and miscellaneous savory vegetable dishes that are often served for breakfast in Sweden. Our version—you guessed it—riffs on the classic presentation by serving tinned salmon in lieu of cured salmon. Simply lay all the components out on your morning table, accompanied by an obligatory hot pot of coffee, and allow your guests to pick and choose the toppings for their own little open-faced-sandwich adventure.

**SERVES 4**

4 slices dense Scandinavian rye bread

4 slices crispbread

1 tin Fishwife Smoked Atlantic Salmon

½ cucumber, thinly sliced

4 hard-boiled eggs, sliced

Salted butter, for the table

1 wedge of aged Alpine-style cheese, such as Emmental, Gruyère, or Comté

Dill sprigs

The instructions for this dish are as simple as presenting all the ingredients on the table and digging in!

RECIPE NOTE: The following are some suggestions for assembling the ultimate bite.

- Rye bread, butter, cucumber, and smoked salmon
- Crispbread, butter, hard-boiled egg, smoked salmon, and dill
- Rye bread, butter, sliced cheese, and cucumber slices

# POTATO, CARAMELIZED ONION, AND TROUT HASH WITH HERBED YOGURT

A good hash sits close to the top of our preferred savory breakfast chart. The combination of small crispy potatoes, gently caramelized onion, and smoky trout satisfies our usual craving for something deeply savory in the mornings, and the tangy and herbaceous yogurt helps to balance the richness of the dish—making it versatile enough to eat as a nourishing breakfast for one or as a decadent brunch for many.

**SERVES 4**

1 garlic clove

2 teaspoons fresh lemon juice

½ cup plain full-fat Greek yogurt

1 tablespoon chopped fresh parsley

1 tablespoon chopped fresh dill

1 tablespoon chopped fresh chives

Fine sea salt and freshly ground black pepper

3 tablespoons extra virgin olive oil

5 to 6 golf-ball-size potatoes, cut into ½-inch dice

½ large red onion, thinly sliced

1 teaspoon dried oregano

½ teaspoon Aleppo pepper or other mild, fruity ground chile

1 or 2 tins Fishwife Smoked Rainbow Trout, flaked into bite-size pieces

4 large eggs

Use a Microplane to grate the garlic into a small bowl. Cover with the lemon juice and set aside to macerate for 5 minutes. Add the yogurt, parsley, dill, chives, and a pinch each of salt and black pepper. Mix well to combine and set aside.

Heat a large, heavy-bottomed skillet over medium heat. Add the olive oil. When the oil is quite hot but not smoking, add the potatoes. Season with a small pinch of salt and toss to properly coat the potatoes. Cook, stirring occasionally, until the potatoes have gently browned, 8 to 10 minutes. Add the onion slices, oregano, and Aleppo pepper, and season with another pinch of salt. Continue cooking until the onion has also started to take on a bit of color, 5 to 8 minutes. If, at this point, your potatoes aren't fork-tender, place a lid on the pan to trap in a bit of steam, reduce the heat, and continue cooking until the potatoes are cooked through. Remove from the heat and fold in the smoked trout.

Fry the eggs in whatever style you prefer.

To serve, smear a generous puddle of the herbed yogurt on the bottom of individual plates. Pile on the potatoes, and top each serving with a fried egg.

# SAVORY MISO OATS WITH CHILI CRISP SALMON

This one is for everybody who loves porridge but dislikes a sweet breakfast. The steel-cut oats are cooked until tender in ginger-scented coconut milk, then seasoned with a heaping tablespoon of light miso. This is a great make-ahead dish—cook up a big batch on the weekend for a week's worth of easy breakfasts. Simply heat up your premade porridge and adorn it with some chili crisp salmon, a jammy egg, and a showering of sliced scallion.

**SERVES 2**

1 tablespoon unsalted butter

¾ cup steel-cut oats

¾ cup full-fat coconut milk

1 teaspoon grated fresh ginger

1 heaping tablespoon light miso

Flaky sea salt

1 tin Fishwife Smoked Salmon with Sichuan Chili Crisp, oil reserved

2 Perfectly Jammy Eggs (page 11)

1 scallion, thinly sliced, for garnish

Lime wedges, for serving

In a small saucepan, heat the butter over medium heat. When it's melted and beginning to foam, add the oats. Stir the oats to ensure they're evenly coated in butter and gently toast until they're deeply aromatic. Then add the coconut milk and 1 cup of water. Bring the mixture to a boil, then reduce the heat to a gentle simmer. Cook, stirring occasionally, for 25 minutes or so, until the oats are just tender.

When the oats are cooked to your liking, stir in the grated ginger. Place the miso in a small bowl and ladle in a couple spoonfuls of the cooked oats. Stir this mixture together to properly incorporate the miso, then return it to the pot with the rest of your oats. Stir to combine and season with a generous pinch of flaky sea salt.

To serve, scoop the oats into bowls and top each serving with chili crisp salmon and a jammy egg and garnish with the sliced scallion. Finish with a generous squeeze of lime and a drizzle of the oil from the salmon tin.

RECIPE NOTE: While you might be tempted to add more liquid to the oats toward the end of their cook time, we urge you to wait until after you've added the miso before you decide the porridge is too thick. Miso has a tendency to make whatever you're adding it to thinner, and if you've already thinned the porridge, you'll likely find yourself disappointed with the end result, which will be more like a loose oat soup than the luscious bowl of oatmeal we're going for.

# OEUFS MAYO

Oeufs mayonnaise is a classic French dish of hard-boiled eggs drenched in a seasoned mayonnaise, often served with some freshly cut chives and a couple leaves of crisp lettuce. Our version riffs on the classic—we opt for a jammier soft-boiled egg, season our mayo with garlic (essentially making aioli), and drape each halved egg with a meaty anchovy. Enjoy alongside Olive Oil Fried Bread (page 4) and A Simple Green Salad (page 10).

**SERVES 2**

¼ cup Aioli (page 3)

4 Perfectly Jammy Eggs (page 11), halved

Flaky sea salt

Aleppo pepper

8 oil-packed Fishwife Cantabrian Anchovies

Chopped fresh chives, for garnish

Smear a generous amount of aioli on a plate. Place the halved eggs on top and season generously with flaky sea salt and a small pinch of Aleppo pepper. Drape an anchovy over each egg half, then shower chives over the tops.

# DEEP DIVE
## THE ART OF THE TOAST

NOTHING BEATS THE CRUNCH OF TOASTED BREAD FRIED IN OLIVE OIL, THE CREAMY BITE OF A BUTTER SCHMEAR, AND THE SALTY KICK OF TINNED FISH.

## BREAD
SOURDOUGH TOAST, RYE, BAGUETTE, CIABATTA

## TINNED FISH
SALMON, TROUT, SARDINES, TUNA, ANCHOVIES, MACKEREL

## FAT
BUTTER, OLIVE OIL, SOFT CHEESE

## VEGGIE
TOMATO, AVOCADO, CUCUMBER, GARLIC, PICKLED VEGGIES

## SEASONING
SEA SALT, BLACK PEPPER, FURIKAKE, WHITE PEPPER, CHILE FLAKES, URFA CHILE, ALEPPO PEPPER

## ACID
SQUEEZE OF LEMON OR LIME, OR VINEGAR

# LATKES WITH SOUR CREAM, CHIVES, AND SMOKED MACKEREL

There's nothing quite like the satisfaction of a deeply golden crispy latke, especially when served with sour cream and chives. How to make the experience all the more luxurious? Eat them with a tin of smoked mackerel. And better yet? Eat them for breakfast!

**SERVES 4 TO 6**

2 pounds russet potatoes
  (approximately
  3 or 4 large potatoes)

1 large yellow onion

2 large eggs

¼ cup panko
  breadcrumbs

2 teaspoons fine sea salt

1½ teaspoons baking
  powder

¼ teaspoon freshly
  ground black pepper

Grapeseed oil, for frying

Flaky sea salt

½ cup sour cream

3 tablespoons finely
  sliced fresh chives

2 tins Fishwife Slow
  Smoked Mackerel

Grate the potatoes and onion on the largest holes of a box grater. Place the grated potatoes and onion on a tea towel and wring out as much liquid as possible. Transfer the potato and onion mixture to a medium bowl.

In a small bowl, whisk the eggs. Add in the panko, fine sea salt, baking powder, and black pepper. Add three-quarters of this mixture to the potatoes and mix well to coat. You want the surface of the potatoes to be slightly tacky and well coated in the mixture, but you don't want them wet or soupy. If the mixture feels too dry, add the remaining quarter of the egg mixture. The potatoes should stick together when squeezed between your fingers.

Line a baking sheet with paper towels. (If making these for a crowd, set a wire rack over another baking sheet. Transferring the latkes from the paper towel to a wire rack will ensure that they stay crunchy as you cook the rest. It also allows you to easily pop the baking sheet and wire rack into a 250°F oven to warm them through before serving.)

**RECIPE CONTINUES >**

Heat a large, heavy-bottomed skillet over medium heat. When hot but not smoking, add enough oil to coat the bottom with a height of approximately ¼ inch and heat until shimmering. Add a small bit of the potato mixture to test if the oil is hot enough; it should sizzle on contact. Drop spoonfuls of the latke mixture into the hot oil and press them down with the flat edge of a spatula. Take care not to crowd the pan. Fry until golden brown and cooked through, about 2 minutes per side. Transfer to the paper towel–lined baking sheet and sprinkle with flaky sea salt.

Serve immediately, with the sour cream, chives, and smoked mackerel.

# SMOKED SALMON FRITTATA WITH FETA CHEESE AND DILL

This frittata is in equal parts a celebration of the endless versatility of tinned fish as it is of the briny, salty delight that is a hunk of feta cheese. Both take center stage in making this frittata the delectable dish that it is. While we recommend serving it alongside A Simple Green Salad (page 10) for breakfast, it would be equally fitting as a light lunch or for a picnic.

**SERVES 4 TO 6**

8 large eggs

¾ teaspoon fine sea salt, plus more to season

½ teaspoon freshly ground black pepper

½ cup feta cheese, crumbled into large pieces

2 tins Fishwife Smoked Atlantic Salmon

¼ cup extra virgin olive oil

½ medium yellow onion, finely diced

3 heaping cups spinach

3 tablespoons coarsely chopped fresh dill

1 tablespoon coarsely chopped fresh tarragon

¼ teaspoon Aleppo pepper

Flaky sea salt

Lemon wedges, for serving

A Simple Green Salad (page 10, optional)

Preheat the oven to 350°F.

In a large bowl, combine the eggs, fine sea salt, and black pepper and whisk very well. Crumble in the feta, flake in the salmon, and gently mix to combine.

In a medium ovenproof nonstick pan, heat the olive oil, onion, and a small pinch of fine sea salt over medium heat. Cook until the onion has softened and released its sweetness, about 5 minutes. Add the

**RECIPE CONTINUES >**

spinach, 2 tablespoons of the dill, and the tarragon to the pan. Cook, turning the spinach with tongs to coat it in the oniony olive oil, until the spinach has fully wilted and the herbs smell aromatic. Season with another small pinch of fine sea salt.

Pour in the egg mixture, and gently stir to evenly distribute all the ingredients.

Transfer the pan to the oven and bake for 15 minutes, or until the eggs are just set. Remove the pan from the oven and turn on the broiler. Place the pan back in the oven, directly under the broiler, and cook for a minute or two, until the top of the frittata is golden brown.

Remove from the oven. Use a spatula to gently transfer the frittata from the pan to a serving plate, or serve the frittata straight from the pan. Top it with the remaining 1 tablespoon of dill, the Aleppo pepper, and a pinch of flaky sea salt. Serve with lemon wedges and, if desired, a green salad.

# CHILI CRISP SALMON BENEDICT

Just as a luscious hollandaise sauce has the ability to transform the blandest of foods into something magnificent, a tin of our smoked salmon has the ability to uplevel a classic eggs benedict into something even more delicious than the original. Here, we trade the more conventional Canadian bacon for a tin of our chili crisp smoked salmon for an unorthodox but explosively flavorful take on the beloved brunch dish.

**SERVES 2**

### FOR THE HOLLANDAISE SAUCE

½ cup unsalted butter

3 large egg yolks

1 teaspoon Dijon mustard

1 tablespoon fresh lemon juice

Cayenne pepper

Fine sea salt and freshly ground black pepper

### FOR THE EGGS BENEDICT

4 large eggs

1 tablespoon distilled white vinegar, rice vinegar, or white wine vinegar

Flaky sea salt

Freshly ground black pepper

1 tin Fishwife Smoked Salmon with Sichuan Chili Crisp, oil reserved

2 English muffins, toasted and buttered

2 tablespoons finely chopped fresh chives, for garnish

**MAKE THE HOLLANDAISE SAUCE:** In a small saucepan, melt the butter over medium heat. When the butter is melted and hot to the touch, remove the pan from the heat.

In a high-speed blender, blend together the egg yolks, mustard, lemon juice, a small pinch of cayenne

**RECIPE CONTINUES >**

pepper, and a pinch each of fine sea salt and black pepper. With the blender running on low, slowly stream in the hot melted butter until the mixture forms a thick, glossy emulsification. Cover the sauce and keep warm while you prepare the remaining components. If the sauce gets too thick as it sits, thin it out by whisking in a few drops of warm water.

**PREPARE THE EGGS BENEDICT:** Bring a medium pot of water to a boil. Crack each of the eggs into a separate small ramekin or bowl—while this step certainly creates more dishes, it helps to ensure a smooth transition of the eggs into the hot water. When the water is boiling and you have your eggs at the ready, add the vinegar to the water and reduce the heat by a smidge. Transfer the eggs into the water, one at a time, and leave them to poach, undisturbed, for 3 minutes.

Line a plate with paper towels. Use a slotted spoon to remove the poached eggs from the water and place them on the paper towel–lined plate. Season with a generous pinch of flaky sea salt and a grind of black pepper.

To assemble, add a few pieces of chili crisp salmon to each half of the toasted English muffins, and spoon some of the oil from the tin over the top. Gently place a poached egg on each muffin half. Pour a generous spoonful of warm hollandaise over each egg and garnish with a sprinkle of chives.

# ACKNOWLEDGMENTS

First and foremost, thanks to Michele Crim, my wonderful agent, who first sparked the idea of a Fishwife cookbook. Thank you to Sarah Kwak, our incredibly sharp editor, who tied the book together, and the rest of the team at Harvest: Jacqueline Quirk, copyeditor Mark McCauslin, production editor Jeanie Lee, production manager Chris Andrus, and interior designer Tai Blanche. Thanks also to Josh Nissenboim and his team at Fuzzco, who added a magic touch to the design of the book.

This book wouldn't exist without Fishwife, the company, and Fishwife wouldn't exist (in its current iteration) without the immense contributions of our team members and our supplier and cannery partners.

Thank you to the Fishwife team: Jack Henry Delano, Pierre Jamet, Lauren Murphy, Julia Hendrickson, Julia Citrin. Your hard work and dedication allowed me to put focus into the creation of this book.

Thank you to Danny "Danbo" Miller, Fishwife's illustrator and the illustrator for this book. I still can't believe I get you as my lifelong creative partner.

Thanks to our cannery and supplier partners. Fishwife works with the most highly skilled seafood canners around the world to bring American consumers delicious, responsibly sourced tinned fish. We wouldn't have a business without them. Thank you for trusting us to help tell your stories to our customers.

And thanks to you, our community. Since day one, we've been fortunate to enjoy a deep camaraderie and friendship with our customers. We've built this business with your feedback and input every step of the way, and we hope this cookbook can be a friendly companion to you in your kitchens, making it ever easier for you to enjoy tinned fish.

Lastly, thank you to Vilda, whose elegant recipes have gently uplifted each and every Fishwife product and told their story as beautifully as it could be told. We've been so fortunate to work with you for so many years, and have our partnership culminate in this book.

Becca Millstein

# INDEX

**NOTE:** Page references in *italics* indicate photographs of recipes. Page references in **bold** indicate pages where recipes are listed.

## A

Aioli (building block recipe), 3

anchovy(ies)

about, ix, x

Anchovy and Olive Martini, 151–153, *152*

Anchovy Bagna Càuda with Vegetable Crudité, 157

Anchovy Sourdough Breadcrumbs (building block recipe), 9

Caesar Wedge Salad with Anchovy Breadcrumbs, 41

Caramelized Onion and Anchovy Tart, 168–171, *169*

Garlic and Lemon Marinated Anchovies and Castelvetrano Olives, 158, *159*

Grilled Cheese with Pesto and Anchovies, 175–176, *177*

Heirloom Tomato, Nectarine, Whipped Ricotta, Anchovy, and Basil Salad, 76

Heirloom Tomatoes with Garlic Toast and Anchovies, 83

Jansson's Temptation: Potato, Cream, Onion, and Anchovy Gratin, 143–144, *145*

Lamb Bolognese with Cantabrian Anchovies, 129–130

Pantry Pasta with Chickpeas, Capers, Anchovies, and Breadcrumbs, *178*, 179–180

Radish, Butter, and Anchovy Toast, 16, *17*

Tonnato with Charred Broccoli, Pickled Onion, and Anchovy Breadcrumbs, 53–54

Artichoke Snack Plate, Tuna and Preserved, *18*, 19

Asparagus Rice Bowl with Salmon, Toasted Almonds, and Herbs, 47–48, *49*

avocado(s)
Avocado, Sardine, and
Urfa-Spiced Pepita
Salad, 30, *31*
Avocado and Sardine
Toast, 15
Hand Roll with Smoked
Salmon, Avocado, and
Cucumber, 55–57, *56*
Awase Dashi, 34

## B

Bagna Càuda with Vegetable
Crudité, Anchovy, 157
Baguette with Labne,
Pickled Onion, and
Smoked Salmon, *62*, 63
Balsamic and Mustard
Vinaigrette, 64, *65*, 66
Bolognese with Cantabrian
Anchovies, Lamb, 129–130
bowls
Asparagus Rice Bowl
with Salmon, Toasted
Almonds, and Herbs,
47–48, *49*
Deep Dive: The Weeknight
Tinned Fish Bowl, 36
bread. *see also*
breadcrumbs;
sandwiches; toast
about, xvi
Baguette with Labne,
Pickled Onion, and
Smoked Salmon, *62*, 63
Grilled Bread, Spiced
Mackerel Pâté with,
132–134, *133*

Pan Bagnat: Niçoise Salad
Sandwich, 67–69, *68*
Panzanella, Chili Crisp
Salmon, 92–93
breadcrumbs
Anchovy Sourdough
Breadcrumbs (building
block recipe), 9
Caesar Wedge Salad
with Anchovy
Breadcrumbs, 41
Pantry Pasta with Chickpeas,
Capers, Anchovies,
and Breadcrumbs, *178*,
179–180
Tonnato with Charred
Broccoli, Pickled
Onion, and Anchovy
Breadcrumbs, 53–54
Broccoli, Pickled Onion, and
Anchovy Breadcrumbs,
Tonnato with Charred,
53–54
Broccolini, Sardine and
Pesto Pasta with
Charred, *102*, 103–104
brunch, 189–207, **190**
building block recipes, **2**
about, 1
Aioli, 3
Anchovy Sourdough
Breadcrumbs, 9
Olive Oil Fried Bread, 4, *5*
Perfectly Jammy Eggs, 11
Pickled Onion, 7
Seasoned Labne, 6
A Simple Green Salad, 10
Steamed Rice, 8

butter
about, xvi
for conservas boards, 149
Radish, Butter, and
Anchovy Toast, 16, *17*

## C

Caesar Wedge Salad with
Anchovy Breadcrumbs,
41
capers, xvii
Caramelized Onion and
Anchovy Tart, 168–171,
*169*
cheese
Grilled Cheese with
Pesto and Anchovies,
175–176, *177*
Heirloom Tomato,
Nectarine, Whipped
Ricotta, Anchovy, and
Basil Salad, 76
Jansson's Temptation:
Potato, Cream, Onion,
and Anchovy Gratin,
143–144, *145*
Pasta Salad with Tuna,
Roasted Red Peppers,
Feta, Red Onion, and
Kalamata Olives,
73–74, *75*
Potato Salad with Green
Beans, Goat Cheese,
and Smoked Salmon,
64–66, *65*
Smoked Salmon Frittata
with Feta Cheese and
Dill, 202–204, *203*

cheese (*continued*)

Smoked Salmon Mac and
Cheese, 117–119, *118*

Trout Orzo with Kale,
Green Olive, and
Parmesan, 109–110

Cherry Tomato Tartine
with Aioli and Smoked
Salmon, 32, *33*

Chickpeas, Capers,
Anchovies, and
Breadcrumbs, Pantry
Pasta with, *178*, 179–180

chile flakes, xviii

chili crisp salmon

Chili Crisp Salmon
Benedict, 205–207, *206*

Chili Crisp Salmon Burger
with Lettuce, Tomato,
and Mayo, 87–88, *89*

Chili Crisp Salmon Lettuce
Wraps with Pickled Onion
and Cucumber, *78*, 79

Chili Crisp Salmon
Panzanella, 92–93

Foil Dinner with Chili Crisp
Salmon, *126*, 127–128

Maple-Glazed Chili Crisp
Salmon with Steamed
Rice and Scallions,
184, *185*

Savory Miso Oats with
Chili Crisp Salmon,
194–195

Seaweed Snacks with
Chili Crisp Salmon,
Mayo, Scallions, and
Sesame Seeds, 22, *23*

chowder and stew

Deep Dive: An Ode
to Tinned Fish
Chowder, 131

Fisherman's Stew with
Salmon, Mussels,
Cockles, and Saffron
Aioli, 146–147

Smoked Salmon Chowder
with Potatoes and Corn,
140–142, *141*

cockles

Fisherman's Stew with
Salmon, Mussels,
Cockles, and Saffron
Aioli, 146–147

Spaghetti Vongole with
Cockles, 111–113, *112*

cocktail party recipes,
149–171, **150**

cocktails and alcoholic
beverages

Anchovy and Olive
Martini, 151–153, *152*

Deep Dive: The Great
Tinned Fish Beverage
Companion Guide, 156

cold weather recipes,
121–147, **122**

Congee with Smoked
Salmon, Mushroom and
Thyme, 123–125, *124*

conservas board, 149

Crackers, Sardines with
Honey Mustard
and, 20

Crackers, Smoked Salmon
Dip with, 24, *25*

crème fraîche

Salmon with Lemon
Crème Fraîche, 164

Smoked Salmon and
Caramelized Shallot
Pasta with Crème
Fraîche and Kale,
97–98, *99*

Spanish Tortilla with
Smoked Salmon, Crème
Fraîche, and Hot Sauce,
38, *39–40*

Crispy Potatoes with Herbed
Yogurt, Pickled Onion,
and Tinned Trout,
80–82, *81*

Crispy Sunchokes with
Rainbow Trout Jerky
Gems, 154–155

cucumber(s)

Chili Crisp Salmon Lettuce
Wraps with Pickled
Onion and Cucumber,
*78*, 79

Hand Roll with Smoked
Salmon, Avocado, and
Cucumber, 55–57, *56*

Smoked Mackerel with
Smashed Cucumbers
and Dill, 77

**D**

Dan Dan Noodles with
Smoked Salmon,
135–136

Deep Dive

An Ode to Tinned Fish
Chowder, 131

The Art of the Toast, 198
The Five-Minute Snack
    Plate, 21
The Great Tinned Fish
    Beverage Companion
    Guide, 156
A Lovely Picnic in the
    Park, 72
Make a Frozen Pizza Hot
    with Tinned Fish, 105
Tinned Fish and Potato
    Chips, 181
The Weeknight Tinned
    Fish Bowl, 36
Deviled Eggs, Tinned
    Smoked Salmon,
    *160*, 161
dinner, 95–119, **96**

**E**

eggs
    about, xvii
    in Aioli (building block
        recipe), 3
    Chili Crisp Salmon
        Benedict, 205–207,
        *206*
    Oeufs Mayo, *196*, 197
    in Pan Bagnat: Niçoise
        Salad Sandwich,
        67–69, *68*
    Perfectly Jammy Eggs
        (building block
        recipe), 11
    Smoked Salmon Frittata
        with Feta Cheese
        and Dill, 202–204,
        *203*
    soft-boiled, 139
    in Spanish Tortilla with
        Smoked Salmon,
        Crème Fraîche, and
        Hot Sauce, *38*, 39–40
    Tinned Smoked Salmon
        Deviled Eggs, *160*, 161
entertaining. *see also* Deep
    Dive
    cocktail party recipes,
        149–171, **150**
    Sunday morning recipes,
        189–207, **190**
Escabeche, Tinned Mussel,
    *162*, 163
extra virgin olive oil, xiv

**F**

fireplace, meals in front of,
    121–147, **122**
Fisherman's Stew with
    Salmon, Mussels,
    Cockles, and Saffron
    Aioli, 146–147
Fishwife, x–xiii
Foil Dinner with Chili Crisp
    Salmon, *126*, 127–128
Fried Rice with Peas,
    Carrots, Scallions,
    and Smoked Mackerel,
    106–108, *107*
furikake, xix

**G**

Garlic and Lemon
    Marinated Anchovies
    and Castelvetrano
    Olives, 158, *159*

Grilled Cheese with
    Pesto and Anchovies,
    175–176, *177*

**H**

Hand Roll with Smoked
    Salmon, Avocado,
    and Cucumber,
    55–57, *56*
Heirloom Tomato,
    Nectarine, Whipped
    Ricotta, Anchovy,
    and Basil Salad, 76
Heirloom Tomatoes with
    Garlic Toast and
    Anchovies, 83
herbs, xvii
Hollandaise Sauce,
    205–207, *206*

**J**

Jansson's Temptation:
    Potato, Cream, Onion,
    and Anchovy Gratin,
    143–144, *145*
Jerky Gems, Crispy
    Sunchokes with
    Rainbow Trout, 154–155
Juicy Summer Tomatoes
    with Sardines and Caper
    Aioli, *70*, 71

**K**

Kale, Green Olive, and
    Parmesan, Trout Orzo
    with, 109–110
Kewpie mayonnaise,
    xviii

## L

Labne, Pickled Onion, and Smoked Salmon, Baguette with, *62*, 63

Labne, Seasoned (building block recipe), 6

Lamb Bolognese with Cantabrian Anchovies, 129–130

late night snacks, 173–187, **174**

Latkes with Sour Cream, Chives, and Smoked Mackerel, 199–200, *201*

lemons, xv

Lettuce, Tomato, and Mayo, Chili Crisp Salmon Burger with, 87–88, *89*

Lettuce Wraps with Pickled Onion and Cucumber, Chili Crisp Salmon, *78*, 79

Lisbon, tinned fish of, ix–x

## M

mackerel

about, x

Fried Rice with Peas, Carrots, Scallions, and Smoked Mackerel, 106–108, *107*

Latkes with Sour Cream, Chives, and Smoked Mackerel, 199–200, *201*

Smoked Mackerel Udon, 137–139, *138*

Smoked Mackerel with Smashed Cucumbers and Dill, 77

Spiced Mackerel Pâté with Grilled Bread, 132–134, *133*

Maple-Glazed Chili Crisp Salmon with Steamed Rice and Scallions, 184, *185*

Matcha Ochazuke with Smoked Salmon, 34–35

mayonnaise

about, xviii

Chili Crisp Salmon Burger with Lettuce, Tomato, and Mayo, 87–88, *89*

substitute for, 3

meals for one, 27–57, **28**

Miso Oats with Chili Crisp Salmon, Savory, 194–195

Mushroom and Thyme Congee with Smoked Salmon, 123–125, *124*

mussel(s)

Fisherman's Stew with Salmon, Mussels, Cockles, and Saffron Aioli, 146–147

Tinned Mussel Escabeche, *162*, 163

mustard

Balsamic and Mustard Vinaigrette, 64, *65*, 66

Honey Mustard and Crackers, Sardines with, 20

## N

Nachos, Supreme Tinned Fish, *182*, 183

nuts and seeds

about, xvii

Asparagus Rice Bowl with Salmon, Toasted Almonds, and Herbs, 47–48, *49*

Avocado, Sardine, and Urfa-Spiced Pepita Salad, 30, *31*

Radicchio Salad with Fennel, Toasted Walnuts, and Rainbow Trout, 44–46, *45*

Seaweed Snacks with Chili Crisp Salmon, Mayo, Scallions, Sesame Seeds and, 22, *23*

sesame seeds in furikake, xix

## O

Oats with Chili Crisp Salmon, Savory Miso, 194–195

Octopus and Smoked Paprika, Risotto with Tinned, 114–116, *115*

Oeufs Mayo, *196*, 197

olive oil, about, xiv

Olive Oil Fried Bread (building block recipe), 4, *5*

olives

Anchovy and Olive Martini, 151–153, *152*

Garlic and Lemon Marinated Anchovies and Castelvetrano Olives, 158, *159*

Pasta Salad with Tuna,
Roasted Red Peppers,
Feta, Red Onion, and
Kalamata Olives,
73–74, *75*
Trout Orzo with Kale,
Green Olive, and
Parmesan, 109–110
onions and scallions
Baguette with Labne,
Pickled Onion, and
Smoked Salmon, *62*, 63
Caramelized Onion and
Anchovy Tart, 168–171, *169*
Chili Crisp Salmon Lettuce
Wraps with Pickled
Onion and Cucumber,
*78*, 79
Crispy Potatoes with
Herbed Yogurt, Pickled
Onion, and Tinned Trout,
80–82, *81*
Fried Rice with Peas,
Carrots, Scallions, and
Smoked Mackerel,
106–108, *107*
Jansson's Temptation:
Potato, Cream, Onion,
and Anchovy Gratin,
143–144, *145*
Maple-Glazed Chili Crisp
Salmon with Steamed
Rice and Scallions,
184, *185*
Pasta Salad with Tuna,
Roasted Red Peppers,
Feta, Red Onion, and
Kalamata Olives, 73–74, *75*

Pickled Onion (building
block recipe), 7
Potato, Caramelized
Onion, and Trout Hash
with Herbed Yogurt,
192–193
Seaweed Snacks with
Chili Crisp Salmon,
Mayo, Scallions, and
Sesame Seeds, 22, *23*
Smoked Salmon and
Caramelized Shallot
Pasta with Crème
Fraîche and Kale,
97–98, *99*
Tonnato with Charred
Broccoli, Pickled
Onion, and Anchovy
Breadcrumbs,
53–54

**P**

Pan Bagnat: Niçoise
Salad Sandwich,
67–69, *68*
pantry essentials, xiv–xix
Pantry Pasta with Chickpeas,
Capers, Anchovies,
and Breadcrumbs, *178*,
179–180
pasta and noodles
about, xvi
Dan Dan Noodles with
Smoked Salmon,
135–136
Lamb Bolognese with
Cantabrian Anchovies,
129–130

Pantry Pasta with
Chickpeas, Capers,
Anchovies, and
Breadcrumbs, *178*,
179–180
Pasta Salad with Tuna,
Roasted Red Peppers,
Feta, Red Onion, and
Kalamata Olives,
73–74, *75*
Sardine and Pesto Pasta
with Charred Broccolini,
*102*, 103–104
Smoked Mackerel Udon,
137–139, *138*
Smoked Salmon and
Caramelized Shallot
Pasta with Crème
Fraîche and Kale,
97–98, *99*
Smoked Salmon Mac and
Cheese, 117–119, *118*
Spaghetti Vongole with
Cockles, 111–113, *112*
Trout Orzo with Kale,
Green Olive, and
Parmesan, 109–110
Pasta Salad with Tuna,
Roasted Red Peppers,
Feta, Red Onion, and
Kalamata Olives,
73–74, *75*
Peach and Sungold Tomato
Salsa, 90, 91
Peanut Sauce, 135
Perfectly Jammy Eggs
(building block
recipe), 11

Pesto and Anchovies,
Grilled Cheese with,
175–176, *177*
Pesto Pasta with Charred
Broccolini, Sardine and,
*102*, 103–104
Pickled Onion (building
block recipe), 7
potato(es)
Crispy Potatoes with
Herbed Yogurt, Pickled
Onion, and Tinned Trout,
80–82, *81*
Deep Dive: Tinned Fish
and Potato Chips, 181
Jansson's Temptation:
Potato, Cream, Onion,
and Anchovy Gratin,
143–144, *145*
Latkes with Sour Cream,
Chives, and Smoked
Mackerel, 199–200,
*201*
Potato, Caramelized
Onion, and Trout Hash
with Herbed Yogurt,
192–193
Potato Salad with Green
Beans, Goat Cheese,
and Smoked Salmon,
64–66, *65*
Smoked Salmon Chowder
with Potatoes and Corn,
140–142, *141*
in Spanish Tortilla with
Smoked Salmon, Crème
Fraîche, and Hot Sauce,
*38*, 39–40

**Q**
quick snacks, 13–25, **14**

**R**
Radicchio Salad with Fennel,
Toasted Walnuts,
and Rainbow Trout,
44–46, *45*
Radish, Butter, and Anchovy
Toast, 16, *17*
Rainbow Trout Tacos with
Peach and Sungold
Tomato Salsa, 90–91
rice
about, xv
Asparagus Rice Bowl
with Salmon, Toasted
Almonds, and Herbs,
47–48, *49*
Congee with Smoked
Salmon, Mushroom
and Thyme, 123–125,
*124*
Fried Rice with Peas,
Carrots, Scallions, and
Smoked Mackerel,
106–108, *107*
Hand Roll with Smoked
Salmon, Avocado, and
Cucumber, 55–57, *56*
Maple-Glazed Chili Crisp
Salmon with Steamed
Rice and Scallions,
184, *185*
rice batter, in Sardine
Fritto Misto with Charred
Lemon and Aioli,
165–166, *167*

Risotto with Tinned
Octopus and Smoked
Paprika, 114–116, *115*
Steamed Rice (building
block recipe), 8

**S**
salads
Avocado, Sardine, and
Urfa-Spiced Pepita
Salad, 30, *31*
Caesar Wedge Salad
with Anchovy
Breadcrumbs, 41
Heirloom Tomato,
Nectarine, Whipped
Ricotta, Anchovy, and
Basil Salad, 76
Pan Bagnat: Niçoise Salad
Sandwich, 67–69, *68*
Pasta Salad with Tuna,
Roasted Red Peppers,
Feta, Red Onion, and
Kalamata Olives,
73–74, *75*
Potato Salad with Green
Beans, Goat Cheese,
and Smoked Salmon,
64–66, *65*
Radicchio Salad with
Fennel, Toasted
Walnuts, and Rainbow
Trout, 44–46, *45*
A Simple Green Salad
(building block
recipe), 10
Trout Salad Sandwich,
*42*, 43

Tuna with White Bean
Salad, Fennel, and
Preserved Lemon
Vinaigrette, 84–86, *85*
salmon. *see also* chili crisp
salmon; smoked salmon
Asparagus Rice Bowl
with Salmon, Toasted
Almonds, and Herbs,
47–48, *49*
Fisherman's Stew with
Salmon, Mussels, Cockles,
and Saffron Aioli, 146–147
Salmon with Lemon
Crème Fraîche, 164
Tinned Fish Smörgåsbord,
191
sandwiches
Pan Bagnat: Niçoise Salad
Sandwich, 67–69, *68*
Sardine and Marinated
Zucchini Sandwich,
50–52, *51*
Tinned Fish Smörgåsbord,
191
Trout Salad Sandwich,
*42*, 43
A Tuna Melt for the Whole
Family, 100, *101*
sardine(s)
Avocado, Sardine, and
Urfa-Spiced Pepita
Salad, 30, *31*
Avocado and Sardine
Toast, 15
Juicy Summer Tomatoes
with Sardines and Caper
Aioli, *70*, 71

Sardine and Marinated
Zucchini Sandwich,
50–52, *51*
Sardine and Pesto Pasta
with Charred Broccolini,
*102*, 103–104
Sardine Fritto Misto with
Charred Lemon and
Aioli, 165–166, *167*
Sardines with Honey
Mustard and
Crackers, 20
Toast with Sardine
Tapenade, *186*, 187
Savory Miso Oats with
Chili Crisp Salmon,
194–195
sea salt, fine, xiv–xv
sea salt, flaky, xv
seasonal recipes
for cold weather,
121–147, **122**
for summertime, 59–93,
**60–61**
Seasoned Labne (building
block recipe), 6
seaweed
Awase Dashi, 34
in furikake, xix
Hand Roll with Smoked
Salmon, Avocado,
and Cucumber,
55–57, *56*
Seaweed Snacks with
Chili Crisp Salmon,
Mayo, Scallions, and
Sesame Seeds, 22, *23*
seeds. *see* nuts and seeds

Shallot Pasta with Crème
Fraîche and Kale,
Smoked Salmon
and Caramelized,
97–98, *99*
A Simple Green Salad
(building block
recipe), 10
Smoked Mackerel Udon,
137–139, *138*
Smoked Mackerel with
Smashed Cucumbers
and Dill, 77
smoked salmon
about, x
Baguette with Labne,
Pickled Onion, and
Smoked Salmon, *62*, 63
Cherry Tomato Tartine
with Aioli and Smoked
Salmon, 32, *33*
Dan Dan Noodles with
Smoked Salmon,
135–136
Hand Roll with Smoked
Salmon, Avocado,
and Cucumber,
55–57, *56*
Matcha Ochazuke with
Smoked Salmon,
34–35
Mushroom and Thyme
Congee with Smoked
Salmon, 123–125, *124*
Potato Salad with Green
Beans, Goat Cheese,
and Smoked Salmon,
64–66, *65*

smoked salmon (*continued*)

Smoked Salmon and
Caramelized Shallot
Pasta with Crème
Fraîche and Kale,
97–98, *99*

Smoked Salmon Chowder
with Potatoes and Corn,
140–142, *141*

Smoked Salmon Dip with
Crackers, 24, *25*

Smoked Salmon Frittata
with Feta Cheese and
Dill, 202–204, *203*

Smoked Salmon Mac and
Cheese, 117–119, *118*

Spanish Tortilla with
Smoked Salmon, Crème
Fraîche, and Hot Sauce,
*38*, 39–40

Tinned Smoked Salmon
Deviled Eggs, *160*, 161

Smörgåsbord, Tinned
Fish, 191

snacks, late night, 173–187,
**174**

snacks, quick, 13–25, **14**

soft-boiled eggs, 139

solo meals, 27–57, **28**

soups. *see* chowder and
stew

soy sauce, xviii–xix

Spaghetti Vongole with
Cockles, 111–113, *112*

Spanish Tortilla with
Smoked Salmon, Crème
Fraîche, and Hot Sauce,
*38*, 39–40

Spiced Mackerel Pâté
with Grilled Bread,
132–134, *133*

spices
chile flakes, xviii
single-origin, xviii

Steamed Rice (building
block recipe), 8

summertime recipes,
59–93, **60–61**

Sunchokes with Rainbow
Trout Jerky Gems,
Crispy, 154–155

Sunday morning recipes,
189–207, **190**

Supreme Tinned Fish
Nachos, *182*, 183

**T**

Tart, Caramelized Onion and
Anchovy, 168–171, *169*

tinned fish. *see also*
anchovy(ies); chili
crisp salmon; cockles;
Deep Dive; mackerel;
mussel(s); sardine(s);
smoked salmon; trout;
tuna
about, xix

Deep Dive: The Weeknight
Tinned Fish Bowl, 36

Tinned Fish Smörgåsbord,
191

Tinned Octopus and
Smoked Paprika, Risotto
with, 114–116, *115*

Tinned Mussel Escabeche,
*162*, 163

Tinned Smoked Salmon
Deviled Eggs,
*160*, 161

toast
Asparagus Rice Bowl
with Salmon, Toasted
Almonds, and Herbs,
47–48, *49*

Avocado and Sardine
Toast, 15

Deep Dive: The Art of the
Toast, 198

Heirloom Tomatoes
with Garlic Toast and
Anchovies, 83

Radicchio Salad with
Fennel, Toasted
Walnuts, and Rainbow
Trout, 44–46, *45*

Radish, Butter, and
Anchovy Toast, 16, *17*

Toast with Sardine
Tapenade, *186*, 187

tomato(es)
Cherry Tomato Tartine
with Aioli and Smoked
Salmon, 32, *33*

Chili Crisp Salmon
Burger with Lettuce,
Tomato, and Mayo,
87–88, *89*

Heirloom Tomato,
Nectarine, Whipped
Ricotta, Anchovy, and
Basil Salad, 76

Heirloom Tomatoes
with Garlic Toast and
Anchovies, 83

Juicy Summer Tomatoes
with Sardines and Caper
Aioli, *70*, 71
Rainbow Trout Tacos with
Peach and Sungold
Tomato Salsa, 90–91
Tonnato with Charred
Broccoli, Pickled
Onion, and Anchovy
Breadcrumbs, 53–54
trout
about, x
Crispy Potatoes with
Herbed Yogurt, Pickled
Onion, and Tinned Trout,
80–82, *81*
Crispy Sunchokes with
Rainbow Trout Jerky
Gems, 154–155
Potato, Caramelized
Onion, and Trout Hash
with Herbed Yogurt,
192–193
Radicchio Salad with
Fennel, Toasted
Walnuts, and Rainbow
Trout, 44–46, *45*
Rainbow Trout Tacos
with Peach and
Sungold Tomato Salsa,
90–91

Trout Orzo with Kale,
Green Olive, and
Parmesan, 109–110
Trout Salad Sandwich,
*42*, 43
tuna
Pan Bagnat: Niçoise
Salad Sandwich,
67–69, *68*
Pasta Salad with Tuna,
Roasted Red Peppers,
Feta, Red Onion, and
Kalamata Olives,
73–74, *75*
Supreme Tinned Fish
Nachos, *182*, 183
Tonnato with Charred
Broccoli, Pickled
Onion, and Anchovy
Breadcrumbs,
53–54
Tuna and Preserved
Artichoke Snack Plate,
*18*, 19
A Tuna Melt for the Whole
Family, 100, *101*
Tuna with White Bean
Salad, Fennel, and
Preserved Lemon
Vinaigrette,
84–86, *85*

**U**
Urfa-Spiced Pepita Salad,
Avocado, Sardine, and,
30, *31*

**V**
Vegetable Crudité, Anchovy
Bagna Càuda with, 157
vinegars, xv

**W**
whey, 6

**Y**
yogurt
in Baguette with Labne,
Pickled Onion, and
Smoked Salmon, *62*, 63
Crispy Potatoes with Herbed
Yogurt, Pickled Onion, and
Tinned Trout, 80–82, *81*
Potato, Caramelized
Onion, and Trout Hash
with Herbed Yogurt,
192–193
in Seasoned Labne
(building block recipe), 6

**Z**
Zucchini Sandwich, Sardine
and Marinated, 50–52, *51*

# ABOUT THE CREATORS

**Becca Millstein** is the cofounder and CEO of Fishwife Tinned Seafood Co. She cofounded Fishwife in 2020 with a mission to make premium, delicious, and ethically sourced tinned seafood a staple in every American cupboard. Becca is from New Hampshire and currently resides in Los Angeles.

**Vilda Gonzalez** is a recipe developer, writer, and avid cook. Her mission is to rewire our collective relationship to what eating well truly means, through the lens of seasonality, sensuality, and storytelling. Vilda was born in Sweden, where she got her first taste of smoked fish, and currently resides in the Hudson Valley.

**Ren Fuller** is a food and lifestyle photographer based in Los Angeles. She loves cooking and adventuring outdoors with her family and hosting her podcast, *Photo Dump*.

**Danny Miller** is a world-renowned illustrator. He lives in Portland, Oregon, with his wife, Daisy, and dog, Junebug. He enjoys painting, exploring forests, and eating hippie-style health food.